AINS 21 Course Guide

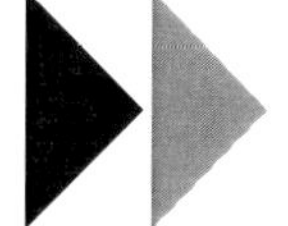

Property and Liability Insurance Principles
6th Edition

The Institutes
720 Providence Road, Suite 100
Malvern, Pennsylvania 19355-3433

6th Edition • 3rd Printing • May 2014

ISBN 978-0-89463-478-9

Contents

Assignments

 **Study Materials Available for AINS 21**

Property and Liability Insurance Principles, 5th ed., 2011, AICPCU.

AINS 21 *Course Guide*, 6th ed., 2011, AICPCU (includes access code for SMART Online Practice Exams).

AINS 21 SMART Study Aids—Review Notes and Flash Cards, 5th ed.

Student Resources

Catalog A complete listing of our offerings can be found in The Institutes' catalog, including information about:

- Current programs and courses
- Current textbooks, course guides, SMART Study Aids, and online offerings
- Program completion requirements
- Exam registration

To obtain a copy of the catalog, visit our website at www.TheInstitutes.org or contact Customer Service at (800) 644-2101.

How to Prepare for Institutes Exams This free handbook is designed to help you by:

- Giving you ideas on how to use textbooks and course guides as effective learning tools
- Providing steps for answering exam questions effectively
- Recommending exam-day strategies

The handbook is printable from the Student Services Center on The Institutes' website at www.TheInstitutes.org or available by calling Customer Service at (800) 644-2101.

Educational Counseling Services To ensure that you take courses matching both your needs and your skills, you can obtain free counseling from The Institutes by:

- Emailing your questions to advising@TheInstitutes.org
- Calling an Institutes' counselor directly at (610) 644-2100, ext. 7601
- Obtaining and completing a self-inventory form, available on our website at www.TheInstitutes.org or by contacting Customer Service at (800) 644-2101

Exam Registration Information As you proceed with your studies, be sure to arrange for your exam.

- Visit our website at www.TheInstitutes.org/forms to access and print the Registration Booklet, which contains information and forms needed to register for your exam.
- Plan to register with The Institutes well in advance of your exam.

How to Contact The Institutes For more information on any of these publications and services:

- Visit our website at www.TheInstitutes.org
- Call us at (800) 644-2101 or (610) 644-2100 outside the U.S.
- Email us at customerservice@TheInstitutes.org
- Fax us at (610) 640-9576
- Write to us at The Institutes, Customer Service, 720 Providence Road, Suite 100, Malvern, PA 19355-3433

Using This Course Guide

This course guide will help you learn the course content and prepare for the exam.

Each assignment in this course guide typically includes the following components:

Educational Objectives These are the most important study tools in the course guide. Because all of the questions on the exam are based on the Educational Objectives, the best way to study for the exam is to focus on these objectives.

Each Educational Objective typically begins with one of the following action words, which indicate the level of understanding required for the exam:

Analyze—Determine the nature and the relationship of the parts.

Apply—Put to use for a practical purpose.

Associate—Bring together into relationship.

Calculate—Determine numeric values by mathematical process.

Classify—Arrange or organize according to class or category.

Compare—Show similarities and differences.

Contrast—Show only differences.

Define—Give a clear, concise meaning.

Describe—Represent or give an account.

Determine—Settle or decide.

Evaluate—Determine the value or merit.

Explain—Relate the importance or application.

Identify or list—Name or make a list.

Illustrate—Give an example.

Justify—Show to be right or reasonable.

Paraphrase—Restate in your own words.

Recommend—Suggest or endorse something to be used.

Summarize—Concisely state the main points.

Outline The outline lists the topics in the assignment. Read the outline before the required reading to become familiar with the assignment content and the relationships of topics.

Key Words and Phrases These words and phrases are fundamental to understanding the assignment and have a common meaning for those working in insurance. After completing the required reading, test your understanding of the assignment's Key Words and Phrases by writing their definitions.

Review Questions The review questions test your understanding of what you have read. Review the Educational Objectives and required reading, then answer the questions to the best of your ability. When you are finished, check the answers at the end of the assignment to evaluate your comprehension.

Application Questions These questions continue to test your knowledge of the required reading by applying what you've studied to "hypothetical" real-life situations. Again, check the suggested answers at the end of the assignment to review your progress.

Sample Exam Your course guide includes a sample exam (located at the back) or a code for accessing SMART Online Practice Exams (which appears on the inside of the cover). Use the option available for the course you're taking to become familiar with the test format.

For courses that offer SMART Online Practice Exams, you can either download and print a sample credentialing exam or take full practice exams using questions like those that will appear on your credentialing exam. SMART Online Practice Exams are as close as you can get to experiencing an actual exam before taking one.

More Study Aids

The Institutes also produce supplemental study tools, called SMART Study Aids, for many of our courses. When SMART Study Aids are available for a course, they are listed on page iii of the course guide. SMART Study Aids include Review Notes and Flash Cards and are excellent tools to help you learn and retain the information in each assignment.

Direct Your Learning 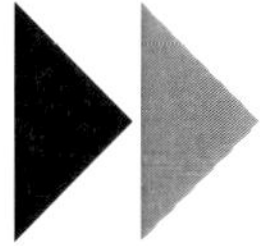

1

Understanding Insurance

After learning the content of this assignment, you should be able to:

1. Explain how insurance functions in each of these roles:
   - As a risk management technique
   - As a transfer system
   - As a business
   - As a contract
2. Distinguish among the common types of personal and commercial insurance.
3. Describe the characteristics of an ideally insurable loss exposure.
4. Explain how insurance benefits individuals, organizations, and society.
5. Describe the costs of insurance.

Outline

▶ **Major Roles of Insurance**
  A. Insurance as a Risk Management Technique
  B. Insurance as a Risk Transfer System
      1. Transferring the Costs of Losses
      2. Sharing the Costs of Losses
  C. Insurance as a Business
  D. Insurance as a Contract

▶ **Common Types of Personal and Commercial Insurance**
  A. Personal Insurance
      1. Property and Liability Insurance
      2. Life and Health Insurance
  B. Commercial Insurance

▶ **Ideally Insurable Loss Exposures**
  A. Pure Risk
  B. Fortuitous Losses
  C. Definite and Measurable
  D. Large Number of Similar Exposure Units
  E. Independent and Not Catastrophic
  F. Affordable

▶ **Benefits of Insurance**
  A. Paying for Losses
  B. Managing Cash Flow Uncertainty
  C. Meeting Legal Requirements
  D. Promoting Risk Control
  E. Enabling Efficient Use of Resources
  F. Providing Support for Insured's Credit
  G. Providing Source of Investment Funds
  H. Reducing Social Burdens

▶ **Costs of Insurance**
  A. Premiums Paid by Insureds
  B. Operating Costs of Insurers
  C. Opportunity Costs
  D. Increased Losses

s.m.a.r.t.® tips Don't spend time on material you have already mastered. The SMART Review Notes are organized by the Educational Objectives found in each assignment to help you track your study.

For each assignment, you should define or describe each of the Key Words and Phrases and answer each of the Review and Application Questions.

Educational Objective 1

Explain how insurance functions in each of these roles:

- **As a risk management technique**
- **As a transfer system**
- **As a business**
- **As a contract**

Key Words and Phrases

Loss exposure

Risk management

Loss prevention

Loss reduction

Exposure unit

Property-casualty insurance

Life-health insurance

Utmost good faith

Contract of adhesion

Contract of indemnity

Self-contained policy

Modular policy

Review Questions

1-1. Identify the general categories of risk management techniques.

1-2. Explain how insurance functions as a system of both transferring and sharing the costs of losses.

1-3. Identify the mechanism through which individuals or businesses exchange the possibility of a large loss for the certainty of a much smaller, periodic payment.

1-4. Explain how the law of large numbers enables insurers to make predictions about losses.

1-5. Identify three prevalent examples of property-casualty insurance.

1-6. What are the primary sources of income for insurers?

Educational Objective 2

Distinguish among the common types of personal and commercial insurance.

Key Words and Phrases

Property insurance

Liability insurance

Homeowners policy

Personal liability coverage

Personal auto policy (PAP)

Comprehensive coverage

Personal watercraft policy

Umbrella liability policy

Liability coverage

Term life insurance

Permanent life insurance

Long-term care insurance

Annuity

Commercial package policy (CPP)

Businessowners policy (BOP)

Commercial auto insurance

Auto physical damage coverage

Commercial property insurance

Ocean marine insurance

Inland marine insurance

Commercial crime insurance

Commercial general liability (CGL) insurance

Professional liability insurance

Workers compensation insurance

Review Questions

2-1. Describe the property coverage provided by a homeowners policy.

2-2. Describe two typical personal liability loss exposures and how a personal umbrella liability policy could provide needed protection

2-3. Distinguish between the two main categories of life insurance.

2-4. Identify the fundamental purpose of an annuity.

2-5. Identify the purpose of commercial package policies and businessowners policies.

2-6. Identify four common causes of loss covered by auto physical damage coverage.

2-7. Identify the purpose of environmental liability insurance.

2-8. Describe the coverage provided by workers compensation insurance.

Educational Objective 3
Describe the characteristics of an ideally insurable loss exposure.

Review Questions

3-1. Distinguish between pure risk and speculative risk.

3-2. Identify the distinguishing characteristic of a fortuitous loss.

3-3. Identify the three components required for an insurer to consider a loss exposure to be definite in the context of ideally insurable loss exposures.

3-4. Explain why an ideally insurable loss exposure must be one of a large number of similar exposure units.

3-5. Identify the distinguishing characteristic of an independent loss exposure.

3-6. Explain why loss exposures involving only small losses and loss exposures involving a high probability of loss are generally considered uninsurable.

Educational Objective 4

Explain how insurance benefits individuals, organizations, and society.

Review Questions

4-1. List the ways insurance benefits individuals, organizations, and society.

4-2. Explain how an organization can achieve risk financing goals through the use of insurance.

4-3. List risk-sharing mechanisms an insurer may use to promote risk control.

Educational Objective 5

Describe the costs of insurance.

Review Questions

5-1. Provide seven examples of an insurer's operating costs.

5-2. Explain how the resources used in the operations of the insurance industry represent opportunity costs.

5-3. What is claim buildup?

5-4. Explain how fraudulent claims increase costs for insureds.

5-5. Explain why the additional losses that result from insureds' carelessness increase the cost of insurance for everyone.

Answers to Assignment 1 Questions

NOTE: These answers are provided to give students a basic understanding of acceptable types of responses. They often are not the only valid answers and are not intended to provide an exhaustive response to the questions.

Educational Objective 1

1-1. Risk management techniques may involve loss avoidance, loss prevention, loss reduction, or risk transfer.

1-2. Insurance is a system of both transferring and sharing the costs of losses because the potential financial consequences of certain loss exposures are transferred to an insurer, which, in turn, pays for covered losses and, in effect, distributes the costs of losses among all insureds (that is, all insureds share the cost of a loss).

1-3. The mechanism through which individuals or businesses exchange the possibility of a large loss for the certainty of a much smaller, periodic payment is an insurance policy.

1-4. The law of large numbers enables insurers to make predictions about losses because according to the law of large numbers, as the number of similar but independent exposure units increases, the relative accuracy of predictions about future outcomes (losses) also increases. Because insurers have large numbers of independent exposure units (the cars and houses of all their insureds, for example), they can predict the number of losses that all similar exposure units combined are likely to experience.

1-5. Prevalent examples of property-casualty insurance include homeowners insurance, automobile insurance, and commercial general liability insurance.

1-6. The primary sources of revenue for insurers are premiums and investment income.

Educational Objective 2

2-1. The property coverage provided by a homeowners policy protects insureds for damage to the home and its contents caused by fire, wind, lightning, and other causes of loss.

2-2. Two typical personal liability loss exposures and how a personal umbrella liability policy could provide needed protection are those in which a jury awards a large sum of money in a liability case and when a homeowner has significant assets to protect and therefore requires higher limits of insurance than those available under personal liability or personal auto coverage.

2-3. There are two main categories of life insurance: term life insurance and permanent life insurance. Term life insurance provides coverage for a specified period, such as ten or twenty years, with no cash value and may be an effective risk management strategy for young families who cannot afford high premiums but need protection for a parent's premature death. Permanent life insurance provides coverage until death, and, in contrast with term life insurance, its premiums remain consistent throughout the life of the policy.

2-4. The fundamental purpose of an annuity is to provide periodic income that an individual cannot outlive.

2-5. The purpose of commercial package policies and businessowers policies is to provide business own-
ers with the necessary property, crime, and liability coverages in one policy.

2-6. Four common causes of loss covered by auto physical damage coverage are collision, fire, theft, and
collision with an animal.

2-7. The purpose of environmental liability insurance is to protect business owners against environ-
mental damage that may occur as a result of business operations.

2-8. Workers compensation insurance pays the cost of medical care, lost wages, and other state-
mandated benefits when employees are injured on the job or acquire a job-related illness, such as
asbestosis.

Educational Objective 3

3-1. Pure risk entails a chance of loss or no loss, but no chance of gain. Conversely, a speculative risk
presents the possibility of loss, no loss, or gain.

3-2. For a loss to be fortuitous, the insured cannot have control over whether or when a loss will occur.

3-3. The three components required for a loss exposure to be definite are time, cause, and location.
The insurer must be able to determine the event (or series of events) that led to the loss, when the
loss occurred, and where the loss occurred.

3-4. An ideally insurable loss exposure must be one of a large number of similar exposure units because
a loss exposure that is one of a large number of similar exposure units allows an insurer to spread
the risk of loss over its entire pool of similar insureds and thereby maintain manageable premium
levels.

3-5. The distinguishing characteristic of an independent loss exposure is that a loss suffered by one
insured does not affect any other insured or group of insureds.

3-6. Loss exposures involving only small losses and loss exposures involving a high probability of loss
are generally considered uninsurable because they are not economically feasible to insure. The
expense of providing the insurance probably exceeds the amount of potential losses.

Educational Objective 4

4-1. Insurance benefits individuals, organizations, and society in these ways:

- Indemnifies individuals and organizations for covered losses
- Enables individuals and organizations to manage cash flow uncertainty
- Enables individuals and organizations to meet legal requirements
- Promotes risk control
- Frees up insured's financial resources for other expenditures or investments
- Supports insured's credit
- Provides source of investment funds for insurers and insureds
- Helps reduce social burden

4-2. Insurance helps an organization achieve risk financing goals in these ways:

- Indemnifies for covered losses—Insurance indemnifies the insured, subject to applicable deductibles and policy limits, for losses to covered loss exposures resulting from covered causes of loss.

- Manages cash flow uncertainty—Insurance helps reduce the financial effect on the insured's cash flow to any deductible payments and any loss amounts that exceed the policy limits.

- Meets legal requirements—Insurance is often used or required to satisfy statutory requirements and contractual requirements that arise from business relationships.

4-3. These risk-sharing mechanisms promote risk control:

- Deductibles

- Premium credit incentives

- Contractual requirements

Educational Objective 5

5-1. Examples of an insurer's operating costs include salaries, producers' commissions, advertising, building expenses, equipment, taxes, and licensing fees.

5-2. The resources used in the operations of the insurance industry represent opportunity costs because capital and labor being used in the insurance industry could be used elsewhere and could create other productive contributions to society.

5-3. Claim buildup is the intentional exaggeration of a loss in an otherwise-legitimate claim.

5-4. Fraudulent claims increase costs for insureds because they pay increased premiums to help cover the costs of those who defraud insurers.

5-5. The additional losses that result from insureds' carelessness increase the cost of insurance for everyone because insurers often pay for injuries and damage that insureds could have prevented.

Direct Your Learning 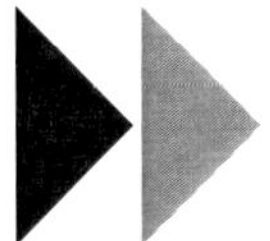

2

Insurers and How They Are Regulated

After learning the content of this assignment, you should be able to:

1. Describe the various types of private insurers that provide property-casualty insurance:

   - Stock insurers
   - Mutual insurers
   - Reciprocal insurance exchanges
   - Lloyd's
   - Captive insurers
   - Reinsurance companies

2. Distinguish among the following insurance functions:

   - Marketing
   - Underwriting
   - Claims
   - Risk control
   - Premium audit

3. Describe United States federal and state government insurance programs in terms of the following:

   - The reasons for these programs
   - The different levels of government involvement in these programs
   - Common examples of federal and state government insurance programs

4. Explain why insurance operations are regulated.

5. Explain how individual states in the United States regulate the licensing of insurers.

2

6. Explain how individual states in the United States regulate insurance rates and policy forms.

7. Explain how the individual states in the United States regulate market conduct and insurer solvency.

8. Explain how the surplus lines insurance market meets the needs of various classes of business that are often unable to find insurance in the standard insurance market.

Outline

▶ **Types of Private Insurers**
  A. Stock Insurers
  B. Mutual Insurers
  C. Reciprocal Insurance Exchanges
  D. Lloyd's
  E. Captive Insurers
  F. Reinsurance Companies

▶ **Overview of Insurance Functions**
  A. Marketing
  B. Underwriting
  C. Claims
  D. Risk Control
  E. Premium Audit

▶ **Government Insurance Programs**
  A. Reasons for Government Insurance Programs
    1. Fill Unmet Needs in the Private Insurance Market
    2. Facilitate Compulsory Insurance Purchases
    3. Provide Efficiency in the Market and Convenience to Insureds
    4. Achieve Collateral Social Purposes
  B. Level of Government Involvement
  C. Common Examples of Federal and State Programs

▶ **Why Insurance Operations Are Regulated**
  A. Protect Consumers
  B. Maintain Insurer Solvency
  C. Prevent Destructive Competition

▶ **Insurer Licensing**
  A. Insurer's Licensing Status
  B. Becoming Licensed as a Domestic Insurer
    1. Forms of Ownership
    2. Capital and Surplus
  C. Becoming Licensed as a Foreign or an Alien Insurer
  D. Admitted Insurers and Nonadmitted Insurers
  E. Producers and Claims Representatives

▶ **Insurance Rate and Form Regulation**
  A. Insurance Rate Regulation
  B. Insurance Policy Form Regulation
  C. Exemptions From Rate and Form Regulation

▶ **Market Conduct and Solvency Regulation**
  A. Market Conduct
    1. Sales and Underwriting
    2. Claims
  B. Insurer Solvency
    1. Establish Financial Requirements
    2. Conduct Field Examinations
    3. Review Annual Statements
    4. Administer IRIS

▶ **The Surplus Lines Market**
  A. Classes of Surplus Lines Business
    1. Unusual or Unique Loss Exposures
    2. Nonstandard Business
    3. Insureds Needing High Limits of Coverage
    4. Insureds Needing Unusually Broad Coverage
    5. Loss Exposures That Require New Forms
  B. Surplus Lines Regulation

Reduce the number of Key Words and Phrases that you must review. SMART Flash Cards contain the Key Words and Phrases and their definitions, allowing you to set aside those cards that you have mastered.

For each assignment, you should define or describe each of the Key Words and Phrases and answer each of the Review and Application Questions.

Educational Objective 1

Describe the various types of private insurers that provide property-casualty insurance:

- **Stock insurers**
- **Mutual insurers**
- **Reciprocal insurance exchanges**
- **Lloyd's**
- **Captive insurers**
- **Reinsurance companies**

Key Words and Phrases

Private insurer

Stock insurer

Mutual insurer

Reciprocal insurance exchange (interinsurance exchange)

Captive insurer, or captive

Reinsurance

Review Questions

1-1. What is the purpose for which a stock insurer is formed?

1-2. What is the role of a stock insurer's board of directors?

1-3. Explain two similarities between mutual insurers and stock insurers regarding earnings.

1-4. Identify five activities an attorney-in-fact of a reciprocal insurance exchange undertakes for the subscribers.

1-5. Identify three reasons why captive insurers became more prevalent in the late 1970s and early 1980s.

Educational Objective 2

Distinguish among the following insurance functions:

- **Marketing**
- **Underwriting**
- **Claims**
- **Risk control**
- **Premium audit**

Key Words and Phrases

Underwriting

Underwriter

Claim

Risk control

Premium audit

Review Questions

2-1. What does marketing involve?

2-2. What is the goal of underwriting when determining the price for insurance?

2-3. What is the purpose of the claims handling process?

2-4. What observations about policyholders might premium auditors be able to refer
      to insurer underwriters because of their direct contact with policyholders?

Educational Objective 3

Describe United States federal and state government insurance programs in terms of the following:

- **The reasons for these programs**
- **The different levels of government involvement in these programs**
- **Common examples of federal and state government insurance programs**

Review Questions

3-1. Identify four main purposes of government insurance programs.

3-2. Provide an example of a government insurance program formed to fulfill an unmet need in the private insurance market.

3-3. Explain why government programs are needed to facilitate compulsory insurance purchases.

3-4. Describe how government insurance programs improve market efficiency.

3-5. Identify the three levels at which the government can participate in an insurance program.

3-6. Provide common examples of federal government insurance programs.

3-7. Provide common examples of state government insurance programs.

Educational Objective 4

Explain why insurance operations are regulated.

Key Word or Phrase

Solvency

Review Questions

4-1. What happens when insurance rates become inadequate due to destructive competition?

4-2. Insurance policy language is usually regulated for what purpose?

4-3. Explain why insurance regulators try to maintain and enhance the financial condition of private insurers.

Educational Objective 5
Explain how individual states in the United States regulate the licensing of insurers.

Key Words and Phrases

Domestic insurer

Foreign insurer

Alien insurer

Admitted insurer

Nonadmitted insurer

Surplus lines law

Review Questions

5-1. What are the three primary forms of an insurer's licensing status in any given state?

5-2. What are the three most common forms of insurer ownership?

5-3. Compare the organization of a stock insurer and a mutual insurer.

5-4. Describe a reciprocal insurance exchange.

5-5. Compare a foreign insurer to an alien insurer.

5-6. Describe a nonadmitted insurer, and explain how nonadmitted insurers can transact business in a state.

5-7. What is the purpose of licensing individual insurance professionals such as producers and claims representatives?

Application Question

5-8. ABC Company is an insurer incorporated and licensed in one state. ABC would like to expand into a neighboring state. What requirements will ABC need to meet in order to be licensed in the neighboring state?

Educational Objective 6
Explain how individual states in the United States regulate insurance rates and policy forms.

Key Words and Phrases

Mandatory rate law

Prior-approval law

File-and-use law

Use-and-file law

Flex rating law

Open competition (no-file law)

Review Questions

6-1. Describe the three major criteria that a state insurance commissioner would consider when deciding to approve or disapprove an insurer's request for a rate.

6-2. Describe how different states meet the three major criteria for insurance rates.

6-3. Compare file-and-use rating laws with use-and-file laws.

6-4. Describe open-competition rating laws.

6-5. What are the two major objectives of regulations regarding insurance policy forms?

6-6. Why are surplus lines insurers generally exempt from insurance regulations pertaining to policy forms and rates?

Application Question

6-7. A new insurer in a state that has an open-competition rating law is charging rates for auto insurance policies that are much lower than those of all of the other auto insurers in the state. Many of the other insurers express concern to the insurance commissioner that these rates are too low.

Discuss whether the insurance commissioner can take action on the complaint in an open-competition rating system. Explain your answer.

Educational Objective 7

Explain how the individual states in the United States regulate market conduct and insurer solvency.

Key Words and Phrases

Market conduct regulation

Unfair trade practices law

Solvency surveillance

National Association of Insurance Commissioners (NAIC)

NAIC Annual Statement

Reserve

Insurance Regulatory Information System (IRIS)

Guaranty fund

Review Questions

7-1.   What is the focus of market conduct regulation?

7-2. Under most state unfair trade practices laws, what penalties can be imposed in each of the following circumstances?

   a. An insurance agent engages in unfair trade practices.

   b. An insurer is guilty of unfair underwriting practices.

7-3. List the four methods regulators use to verify insurers' solvency.

Application Question

7-4. A state insurance department has received several complaints alleging that Insurance Company is slow to resolve claims and then denies them without explanation.

   a. How is the department of insurance likely to follow up on these complaints?

b. This insurance department activity is an example of what type of regulatory oversight?

Educational Objective 8

Explain how the surplus lines insurance market meets the needs of various classes of business that are often unable to find insurance in the standard insurance market.

Key Words and Phrases

Standard market

Surplus lines insurance

Surplus lines insurer

Review Questions

8-1. Identify five classes of business often insured in the surplus lines market.

8-2. Explain why standard market insurers are often unwilling to provide coverage for loss exposures for which a large number of similar exposure units do not exist.

8-3. Explain why the surplus lines market can respond more quickly to immediate needs for new types of coverage than standard market insurers.

8-4. Describe the requirements a surplus lines licensee must fulfill before it can insure a particular risk with a surplus lines insurer.

Answers to Assignment 2 Questions

NOTE: These answers are provided to give students a basic understanding of acceptable types of responses. They often are not the only valid answers and are not intended to provide an exhaustive response to the questions.

Educational Objective 1

1-1. A stock insurer is formed for the purpose of making a profit for its owners.

1-2. A stock insurer's board of directors, which has the authority to control the insurer's activities, creates and oversees corporate goals and objectives and appoints a chief executive officer (CEO) to carry out the insurer's operations.

1-3. These are two examples of the similarities between mutual insurers and stock insurers:

- Mutual insurers generally seek to earn profits in their ongoing operations, as do stock insurers.

- A stock insurer may choose to share profits with its stockholders by the payment of dividends, which are a return on the stockholders' investment. Mutual insurers also may opt to share profits, but pay dividends instead to policyholders as a return of a portion of premiums paid.

1-4. In a reciprocal insurance exchange, an attorney-in-fact acts on behalf of the subscribers to market and underwrite insurance coverage, collect premiums, invest funds, and handle claims.

1-5. These are three reasons why captive insurers became more prevalent in the late 1970s and early 1980s:

- They might provide a lower insurance cost than other private insurers.

- They help ease the problems of availability and affordability for a parent company with loss exposures that may be difficult to insure.

- They can provide improved cash flow that results when the corporation invests funds instead of paying premiums to an unrelated insurer.

Educational Objective 2

2-1. Marketing involves determining the products or services customers want and need and delivering them to those customers.

2-2. The goal of underwriting is to charge a premium that is commensurate with the loss exposure. In other words, each insured's premium should be set at a level that is adequate to enable the total premiums paid by a large group of similar insureds to pay losses and expenses of that group and to allow the insurer to achieve a reasonable profit.

2-3. The purpose of the claims handling process is to achieve a fair and equitable settlement based on the circumstances of the loss.

2-4. Premium auditors can notify underwriters of larger loss exposures than originally contemplated, unacceptable operations, new products, new operations, or financial problems.

Educational Objective 3

3-1. Government insurance programs exist to fill unmet needs in the private insurance market, to facilitate compulsory insurance purchases, to provide efficiency in the market and convenience to insureds, and to achieve collateral social purposes.

3-2. An example of a government insurance program formed to fulfill an unmet need in the private insurance market is the Terrorism Risk Insurance Program (TRIP). The program was intended as a temporary provider of reinsurance for losses caused by terrorism and was designed to run until the end of 2005, but was subsequently extended because the private market for terrorism insurance and reinsurance was not deemed adequate to let it expire as originally anticipated.

3-3. Government programs are needed to facilitate compulsory insurance purchases because not everyone required to purchase such insurance can obtain coverage at a reasonable price in the private market.

3-4. Government insurance programs improve market efficiency by reducing either the time or the resources insureds need to expend to obtain the desired insurance coverage.

3-5. The government can participate in an insurance program as an exclusive insurer, as a partner with a private insurer, or as an insurer in direct competition with private insurers.

3-6. Common examples of federal government insurance plans include the National Flood Insurance Program (NFIP), the Terrorism Risk Insurance Program (TRIP), and federal crop insurance.

3-7. Examples of state government insurance programs include workers compensation plans, residual auto plans, and beach and windstorm plans.

Educational Objective 4

4-1. When insurance rate levels become inadequate, some insurers may not collect enough money to pay all of their insureds' claims and may become insolvent. Other insurers might lose so much profit that they withdraw from the market or stop writing new business. An insurance shortage can then develop, and individuals and organizations might be unable to obtain the coverage they need.

4-2. Regulators review insurance language to protect consumers. Many insurance policies are complex legal documents that may be difficult for some consumers to analyze and understand. Regulators can set coverage standards, specify policy language for certain insurance coverages, and disapprove unacceptable policies.

4-3. Insurance regulators try to maintain and enhance the financial condition of private insurers for several reasons:

- Premiums are paid in advance, and the period of protection extends into the future. If an insurer becomes insolvent, future claims might not be paid even though the premium has been paid. Consumers may find it difficult to evaluate insurers' financial ability to keep their promises.

- Regulation is needed to protect the public interest. Large numbers of individuals are adversely affected when insurers become insolvent. For example, an unusually large catastrophe that affects a large area can make an insurer's financial ability to pay claims uncertain, such as when Hurricane Andrew struck Florida in 1992 and caused seven insurer insolvencies.

- Insurers hold substantial funds for the ultimate benefit of policyholders. Government regulation is necessary to safeguard such funds.

Educational Objective 5

5-1. An insurer's licensing status in any given state may assume that of a domestic insurer, a foreign insurer, or an alien insurer.

5-2. The three most common forms of insurer ownership are stock insurance companies, mutual insurance companies, and reciprocal insurance exchanges.

5-3. Stockholders supply the capital needed to form a stock insurer or to expand its operations. Stockholders expect to receive a return on their investment in the form of stock dividends, increased stock value, or both. A mutual insurer is owned by its policyholders. Because a traditional mutual insurer issues no common stock, it has no stockholders. Stockholders and policyholders have similar voting rights and elect the insurer's board of directors.

5-4. A reciprocal insurance exchange consists of a series of private contracts in which subscribers, or members of the group, agree to insure each other.

5-5. A foreign insurer is a United States insurer that is licensed to do business in a state but is incorporated in a different state. An alien insurer is a non-U.S. insurer that is licensed to do business in the U.S. states where it wishes to operate.

5-6. A nonadmitted insurer, often referred to as a surplus lines insurer, is not authorized by the state insurance department to do business within that state. Under surplus lines laws, a nonadmitted insurer may be permitted to transact business only through a specially licensed surplus lines producer.

5-7. The examinations required for licensing, along with continuing education requirements, attempt to ensure that insurance professionals have a minimum level of insurance knowledge and meet ethical standards.

5-8. ABC will first need to show the regulator in the neighboring state that it has satisfied the requirements in its home state. ABC will also need to satisfy the minimum capital, surplus, and other requirements imposed on domestic insurers within the neighboring state.

Educational Objective 6

6-1.   A state insurance commissioner would consider whether the rate is adequate; it should be sufficient to pay all claims and the expenses related to those claims, helping to maintain insurer solvency. The commissioner would also determine whether or not the rate is excessive and would disapprove an excessive rate; insurers are entitled to a fair return, but not to excessive or unreasonable profit. A state insurance commissioner would also consider whether the rate is unfairly discriminatory; insurers are permitted to adjust premium rates based on the risk profile of different groups of insureds, but these rates must be fair and consistent.

6-2.   Different states meet these criteria by different types of rating laws that vary in the type and extent of control the states assert over insurers' rates.

6-3.   Under file-and-use-laws, insurers must file rates with the state insurance department prior to their use, but the rates can be used immediately without specific approval. Use-and-file laws are a variation of the file-and-use law in which insurers file rates within a specified period of time after the rates are put into use.

6-4.   In open-competition rating, market prices driven by the economic laws of supply and demand, rather than regulatory decisions, determine insurance rates. However, state insurance departments typically have the authority to monitor competition and disapprove rates if deemed necessary. The major criteria that rates must be adequate, not excessive, and not unfairly discriminatory continue to apply.

6-5.   The first objective is that insurance policies be clear and readable to insurance consumers. The second major objective is to detect and address any policy provisions that are unfair or unreasonable.

6-6.   Surplus lines insurers are willing to provide coverage for risks that admitted insurers are unable or unwilling to offer. Because these insurers increase the availability of insurance, they have the freedom to use policy provisions and rates that are appropriate for a particular risk.

6-7.   One of the three major criteria that states consider in evaluating insurance rates is whether they are adequate. Under open-competition rating laws, the insurance commissioner has the responsibility to be sure that rates are adequate, not excessive, and not unfairly discriminatory. Therefore, the insurance commissioner can investigate the rates charged by the new insurer and take action if deemed necessary.

Educational Objective 7

7-1.   Market conduct regulation focuses on insurers' treatment of applicants for insurance, insureds, and others who present claims for coverage.

7-2.   These penalties can be imposed under most state unfair trade practices laws:

a.   State regulators can suspend or revoke the licenses of sales agents or brokers who engage in unfair trade practices.

b.   An insurer that is guilty of unfair underwriting practices could be fined, or its operating license in a state could be suspended or revoked.

7-3. Regulators use these four methods to verify the solvency of insurers:

- Establish financial requirements by which to measure solvency

- Conduct on-site field examinations to ensure regulatory compliance

- Review annual financial statements

- Administer the Insurance Regulatory Information System (IRIS)

7-4. The following answers relate to the state insurance department's response to complaints against Insurance Company.

a. The insurance department may investigate the complaints and may hold a formal hearing as part of the investigation process. If the investigation indicates that the allegations are true, the department may assess a fine against Insurance Company.

b. This insurance department activity is an example of regulating market conduct.

Educational Objective 8

8-1. Five classes of business often insured in the surplus lines market are unusual or unique loss exposures, nonstandard business, insureds needing high limits of coverage, insureds needing unusually broad coverage, and loss exposures that require new forms.

8-2. Standard market insurers are often unwilling to provide coverage for loss exposures for which a large number of similar exposure units do not exist because coverage for such loss exposures is hard to price.

8-3. The surplus lines market can respond quickly to immediate needs for new types of coverage because standard market insurers often take longer to analyze the need for new or revised coverage and to file policy forms and rates for state approval.

8-4. Before it can insure a particular risk, a surplus lines licensee must document that a diligent search for coverage in the standard (admitted) market has been performed.

Direct Your Learning 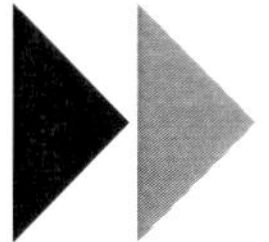

3

Insurer Financial Performance

After learning the content of this assignment, you should be able to:

1. Explain how the management of a property-casualty insurer's income and expenses determines its profitability.

2. Describe the typical items found on the balance sheet and the income statement of a property-casualty insurer.

3. Analyze a property-casualty insurer's profitability information using these financial ratio calculations:

   - Loss ratio

   - Expense ratio

   - Combined ratio

   - Investment income ratio

   - Overall operating ratio

4. Given a case regarding a property-casualty insurer's financial ratio calculation(s), determine the significance of those calculation(s) on the insurer's overall financial performance.

Outline

▶ **Insurer Profitability and Income and Expense Management**

  A. Managing Insurer Income

      1. Underwriting Income

      2. Investment Income

  B. Managing Insurer Expenses

      1. Underwriting Activity Expenses

      2. Investment Activity Expenses

  C. Insurer Profitability

▶ **Understanding Insurer Financial Statements**

  A. Balance Sheet

      1. Assets

      2. Liabilities

      3. Policyholders' Surplus

  B. Income Statement

▶ **Analyzing Insurer Financial Ratio Calculations**

  A. Loss Ratio

  B. Expense Ratio

  C. Combined Ratio

  D. Investment Income Ratio

  E. Overall Operating Ratio

▶ **Knowledge to Action: Financial Ratios and Insurer Financial Performance Case**

  A. Overview of the Procedure

  B. Examine the Loss Ratio

  C. Examine the Expense Ratio

  D. Analyze the Combined Ratio

Actively capture information by using the open space in the SMART Review Notes to write out key concepts. Putting information into your own words is an effective way to push that information into your memory.

For each assignment, you should define or describe each of the Key Words and Phrases and answer each of the Review and Application Questions.

Educational Objective 1

Explain how the management of a property-casualty insurer's income and expenses determines its profitability.

Key Words and Phrases

Loss adjustment expense (LAE)

Paid losses

Incurred losses

Incurred but not reported (IBNR) losses

Dividends

Review Questions

1-1. Identify and describe the two primary sources of an insurer's income.

1-2. Describe the components of each of these types of insurer expenses: (1) underwriting activity expenses and (2) investment activity expenses.

1-3. What financial components determine an insurer's net income before taxes?

Application Question

1-4. The Information Technology (IT) Department for QualitIn Insurance Company was concerned to learn that QualitIn had an underwriting loss for the third year in a row. What might the IT Department do to help improve QualitIn's underwriting profitability? Identify the component(s) of income or expenses that would be affected by the IT Department's action(s).

Educational Objective 2

Describe the typical items found on the balance sheet and the income statement of a property-casualty insurer.

Key Words and Phrases

Assets

Admitted assets

Nonadmitted assets

Liabilities

Loss reserve

Unearned premium reserve

Policyholders' surplus

Review Questions

2-1. The balance sheet shows an insurer's financial position at a particular point in time and includes what three financial components?

2-2. Explain why an unearned premium reserve is an insurer's liability.

2-3. The income statement compares an insurer's revenue generated with the expenses incurred to produce that revenue and includes which financial components?

Application Question

2-4. Before placing a new customer's commercial property insurance with Hallidy Insurance, a company with which he was less familiar, Jerry asked his assistant to retrieve a current balance sheet for Hallidy. The assistant returned with a balance sheet dated four years prior to the current date. Explain why Jerry should avoid basing his decision on placing coverage with Hallidy solely on a four-year-old balance sheet.

Educational Objective 3

Analyze a property-casualty insurer's profitability information using these financial ratio calculations:

- **Loss ratio**
- **Expense ratio**
- **Combined ratio**
- **Investment income ratio**
- **Overall operating ratio**

Key Words and Phrases

Loss ratio

Expense ratio

Combined ratio

Investment income ratio

Review Questions

3-1. Given an insurer with a loss ratio greater than its preestablished target ratio, what is an example of an analysis it might make in finding ways to reduce its total incurred losses?

3-2. An insurer wants to take action to better meet its target expense ratio. Identify one action an insurer might take to improve each of these components of the expense ratio.

a. Written premium

b. Acquisition costs

c. General expenses

3-3. The insurance industry as a whole experiences difficulty in one year because of excessive expenses related to catastrophe losses and a poor economic environment.

a. How might that affect the average combined ratio for the industry?

b. In that same difficult year, two insurers had combined ratios that were less than 100. What would this indicate about those two insurers?

Application Question

3-4. Tamarado Insurance Company, a commercial property, liability, and workers compensation insurer, ended the past year with a combined ratio of 107 percent and an overall operating ratio of 88 percent. Answer the following questions about Tamarado's profitability.

a. What do these ratios indicate about Tamarado's profitability for that year?

b. Suggest two actions that Tamarado might take to improve its profitability for the coming year.

Educational Objective 4

Given a case regarding a property-casualty insurer's financial ratio calculation(s), determine the significance of those calculation(s) on the insurer's overall financial performance.

Application Questions

4-1. Juniquote Insurance set a goal to improve its loss ratio by 15 percent over the next year. Analyze the following proposals and determine whether each would be likely to improve Juniquote's loss ratio.

   a. Juniquote will offer loss control services for its commercial insureds that exceed the services offered by its competitors.

   b. Juniquote will discontinue writing homeowners insurance in two states that have the highest licensing fees (of those states where they write homeowners) and strict requirements for wording that must be used in homeowners policy provisions and all policy-related communications.

4-2. Sauguine Insurance hired an experienced investment manager to select profitable investments and to balance its investment portfolio and still meet regulatory requirements for its use of policyholders' surplus.

   How might Sauguine's hire of this investment manager improve its overall gain or loss from operations?

4-3.   Overlan Insurance writes a high volume of personal auto insurance throughout the United States. Because Overlan specializes in auto insurance, it offers a lower premium than any other auto insurer. Overlan is reviewing its loss ratio, expense ratio, and combined ratio to find ways to improve its combined ratio of 106 percent. The combined ratio was calculated using these figures:

$$\text{Combined ratio} = \text{loss ratio} + \text{expense ratio}$$

$$106\% = 68\% + 38\%$$

Evaluate whether each of these proposals, in absence of other proposals, could significantly improve Overlan's combined ratio, and explain your answer.

a.   Overlan will offer a 10 percent rate decrease for all of its new and existing policyholders.

b.   Overlan will implement a new cost-effective system that enables prospective insureds to submit an online application for insurance. The system evaluates the risk and provides a quote to the insured in two minutes or less. The system also enables insureds to accept the quote, renew their policy online, make online premium payments, and submit most policy changes to Overlan online.

Answers to Assignment 3 Questions

NOTE: These answers are provided to give students a basic understanding of acceptable types of responses. They often are not the only valid answers and are not intended to provide an exhaustive response to the questions.

Educational Objective 1

1-1. An insurer's income is primarily composed of underwriting income and investment income. Underwriting income is generated by the sale of insurance and is the amount remaining (either a gain or a loss) after underwriting losses and expenses are subtracted from earned premiums. Investment income is generated from the insurer's investment of funds and is the amount remaining (either a gain or a loss) after investment expenses are subtracted from the gross amount earned on investments during a period.

1-2. These answers describe the components of two types of insurance expenses.

- Underwriting activity expenses include the insurer's paid and incurred losses, loss adjustment expenses, and other underwriting expenses, including acquisition expenses, general expenses (expenses associated with staffing and maintaining functional departments), and premium taxes, licenses, and fees.

- Investment activity expenses include staff salaries of professional investment managers and all other expenses related to the investment department's activities.

1-3. An insurer's net income before taxes is the sum of its total earned premiums and investment income minus its total losses and other expenses in the corresponding period, with any applicable adjustments.

1-4. Because the IT Department is not involved in underwriting, which directly affects premiums, or in claims, which directly affect losses and loss expenses, the best way for the IT Department to help improve QualitIn's underwriting profitability is to look for ways to cut expenses within its own department or to suggest ways to cut expenses for the entire organization. These expenses are general expenses of the insurer, which are a component of "other underwriting expenses." Any actions that reduce expenses will help lead to greater profitability.

Educational Objective 2

2-1. The balance sheet includes the insurer's assets, liabilities, and policyholders' surplus.

2-2. The unearned premium reserve is a liability because it represents insurance premiums prepaid by insureds for services that the insurer has not yet rendered. If the insurer ceased operations and canceled all of its policies, the unearned premium reserve would represent the total of premium refunds that the insurer would owe its current policyholders.

2-3. The income statement includes the insurer's revenue (earned premiums), expenses (incurred losses, loss adjustment expenses, and other underwriting expenses), net underwriting gain or loss, net investment income, and net income before income taxes.

2-4. An insurer's balance sheet shows its assets and liabilities only as of a particular date, a snapshot of the insurer's financial position at that point in time. The figures change constantly. Insurers establish unearned premium reserves for premiums they receive. The unearned premium reserve for each policy declines with the passage of time. Also, losses occur, and insurers establish loss reserves. New policies are written, and old policies expire or are renewed. Meanwhile, the insurer buys and sells stocks, bonds, and other investments as needed to meet its obligations while earning investment income. Because of these factors, Hallidy's balance sheet has probably changed considerably in a four-year period. Therefore, Jerry should locate a more recent balance sheet to help with his placement decision, and he may also want an income statement for the corresponding period(s).

Educational Objective 3

3-1. This is one acceptable answer:

To reduce its loss ratio, an insurer could review the types of insurance that it writes and evaluate the loss potential for those types of insurance or the territories where it writes that insurance. It could identify types of insurance or territories that are highly susceptible to losses and consider the effect of reducing the volume of such business, while increasing the volume of business it writes that is less susceptible to losses.

3-2. These are actions an insurer might take to reduce components of the expense ratio: (Answers will vary.)

    a.   The insurer may be able to increase its written premium while managing its growth by staying the course with a plan developed previously to support its growth mode.

    b.   To reduce acquisition costs, the insurer might discontinue a costly and unprofitable agency incentive program.

    c.   To reduce general expenses, the insurer might offer an employee incentive program to encourage employees to work more efficiently and make fewer errors.

3-3. These answers address questions regarding the insurance industry in a poor economic environment:

    a.   The average combined ratio for the industry for that year could be a loss (greater than 100).

    b.   This would indicate that those two insurers had a gain in a very difficult year. Those two insurers would stand out as exceptional insurers in a difficult insurance market.

3-4. These answers address questions regarding the Tamarado case:

    a.   The combined ratio of 107 percent indicates that Tamarado suffered an underwriting loss of 7 percent for that year. For every $1.00 of premium that Tamarado earned, it paid $1.07 for losses and expenses. Tamarado's overall operating ratio of 88 percent indicates that Tamarado's investments for that year were successful and that, in spite of its underwriting loss, Tamarado earned a profit on its investments and, consequently, earned an overall profit for the year.

b.   Tamarado should increase its earned premiums or decrease its expenses to improve its underwriting ratio for the coming year. These actions could help improve its profitability:

- Tamarado could offer an innovative, new service for its commercial insureds and increase its premiums.

- Tamarado could reduce its legal expenses by selecting legal defense counsel that have fees and limitations that conform to the claim department's guidelines.

Educational Objective 4

4-1.   These are possible answers for each of the proposals:

a.   Assuming insureds take advantage of these services and the result is fewer losses or less severe losses, this proposal would decrease Juniquote's losses and, consequently, its loss adjustment expenses, leading to improvement in its loss ratio.

b.   This proposal is not likely to improve Juniquote's loss ratio. Discontinuing writing homeowners insurance in these states may decrease Juniquote's operating expenses because of added processing costs and the need to maintain unique policy forms and communication forms for those two states. However, operating expenses are not a component in an insurer's loss ratio, which probably would not be affected by this proposal.

4-2.   Assuming this investment manager increases Sauguine's net investment income by improving its investment earnings and reducing its investment expenses, Sauguine's improved net investment income would be added to its net underwriting gain or loss to improve its overall gain or loss from operations.

4-3.   These are possible answers for each of the proposals:

a.   In the absence of other proposals, this proposal could generate additional business, which may improve the expense ratio; however, Overlan's current loss ratio of 68 percent is not a problem. Alternately, reducing its premiums in a noncompetitive market could lower its earned premiums and could increase its loss ratio and its expense ratio (premiums are a component of both), and hence its combined ratio.

b.   Provided the system works as specified, this proposal could probably improve Overlan's expense ratio and hence its combined ratio. This system may enable Overlan to reduce its acquisition expenses over time by minimizing or eliminating producer commissions and incentives. The submission, renewal, premium payment, and policy change features of the system could enable Overlan to reduce customer service and accounting staff, which would reduce its general expenses.

B

Direct Your Learning 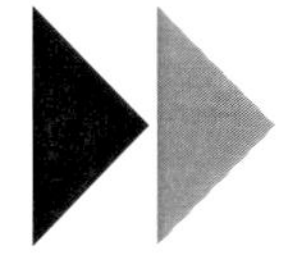

Marketing

Educational Objectives

After learning the content of this assignment, you should be able to:

1. Describe the following factors that influence an agency relationship:

   - Legal roles

   - Legal responsibilities

   - Scope of authority

2. Summarize the various types of insurance distribution systems and alternative marketing channels.

3. Describe the functions performed by insurance producers.

4. Describe the key factors an insurer should evaluate during the distribution-system and distribution-channel selection process.

5. Explain how states regulate insurance marketing activities in these areas:

   - Licensing

   - Compensation

   - Unfair trade practices

Outline

▶ **Understanding Factors That Influence an Agency Relationship**
   A. Legal Roles
   B. Legal Responsibilities
      1. Legal Responsibilities of the Agent to the Principal
      2. Legal Responsibilities of the Principal to the Agent
      3. Responsibilities to Third Parties
   C. Scope of Authority
      1. Actual Authority
      2. Apparent Authority

▶ **Summarizing Types of Insurance Distribution Systems**
   A. Independent Agency and Brokerage Marketing System
      1. Independent Agents and Brokers
      2. National and Regional Brokers
      3. Independent Agency Networks
      4. Managing General Agents
      5. Surplus Lines Brokers
   B. Exclusive Agency Marketing System
   C. Direct Writer Marketing System
   D. Distribution Channels
      1. Internet
      2. Call Centers
      3. Direct Response
      4. Group Marketing
      5. Trade Associations
      6. Financial Institutions
   E. Mixed Marketing System

▶ **Functions of Insurance Producers**
   A. Prospecting
   B. Risk Management Review
      1. Individual or Family
      2. Businesses
   C. Sales
   D. Policy Issuance
   E. Premium Collection
   F. Customer Service
   G. Claims Handling

   H. Consulting

▶ **Distribution System and Channel Selection for Insurance Marketing**
   A. Customers' Needs and Characteristics
   B. Insurer's Profile
      1. Insurer Strategies and Goals
      2. Insurer Strengths
      3. Existing and Target Markets
      4. Geographic Location
      5. Degree of Control Required

▶ **How States Regulate Insurance Marketing Activities**
   A. Licensing
      1. Insurers
      2. Insurance Personnel
   B. Compensation
      1. Sales Commissions
      2. Contingent Commissions
   C. Unfair Trade Practices
      1. Misrepresentation and False Advertising
      2. Tie-In Sales
      3. Rebating
      4. Other Deceptive Practices

Use the SMART Online Practice Exams to test your understanding of the course material. You can review questions over a single assignment or multiple assignments, or you can take an exam over the entire course.

For each assignment, you should define or describe each of the Key Words and Phrases and answer each of the Review and Application Questions.

Educational Objective 1

Describe the following factors that influence an agency relationship:

- **Legal roles**
- **Legal responsibilities**
- **Scope of authority**

Key Words and Phrases

Producer

Agent

Agency

Principal

Actual authority

Express authority

Implied authority

Binding authority

Apparent authority

Review Questions

1-1. Identify three factors that influence an agency relationship.

1-2. What are the two essential elements of an agency relationship?

1-3. Identify the five duties that the laws of agency impose on insurance agents.

1-4. Identify three examples of the rights and duties an agency contract addresses.

1-5. Identify the legal responsibilities of the principal to the agent.

1-6. Identify the two types of actual authority.

Application Question

1-7. Alex owns and manages the Independent Insurance Agency. Alex would like
to begin offering payment plans to his customers who have large insurance
premiums. Alex has made arrangements with a local bank that will finance
the premiums for his customers. How can Alex determine whether this type of
arrangement is acceptable to the insurers that he represents?

Educational Objective 2
Summarize the various types of insurance distribution systems and alternative marketing channels.

Key Words and Phrases

Independent agency

Broker

Agency expiration list

Independent agency network

Managing general agent (MGA)

Exclusive agency marketing system

Direct writer marketing system

Mixed marketing system

Review Questions

2-1. Identify the three main insurance distribution systems.

2-2. Identify an agency's most valuable asset.

2-3. Identify the two typical forms of compensation for independent agents and brokers.

2-4. Identify three examples of administrative functions an exclusive agency insurer handles for the exclusive agent.

2-5. What are two ways in which direct writer insurers can encourage their sales agents to develop new business?

2-6. Explain how insurance portals benefit customers.

2-7. Identify one advantage and one disadvantage of the direct response distribution channel.

2-8. Describe the group marketing technique of affinity marketing.

2-9. Identify the purpose of trade association advertising.

2-10. What qualities of financial institutions make them beneficial strategic partners for insurers?

2-11. Identify three issues that must be considered when using a mixed marketing system.

Educational Objective 3
Describe the functions performed by insurance producers.

Key Words and Phrases
Cold canvass

Loss run

Agency bill

Direct bill

Review Questions

3-1. Name six methods producers use to locate prospective clients.

3-2. Describe the types of information included in a loss run that may be of use to a producer.

3-3. Describe three widely used methods used to transfer premiums to insurers in the agency bill process.

3-4. Identify two advantages of using qualified producers to handle claims.

Educational Objective 4

Describe the key factors an insurer should evaluate during the distribution-system and distribution-channel selection process.

Review Questions

4-1. Name the factors an insurer must evaluate relating to its profile when selecting distribution systems and channels.

4-2. Describe how assessment of its internal strengths and weaknesses can help an insurer in the selection of distribution systems and channels.

4-3. Describe the considerations relating to existing markets that an insurer might evaluate during the process of selecting distribution systems and channels.

Educational Objective 5

Explain how states regulate insurance marketing activities in these areas:

- **Licensing**
- **Compensation**
- **Unfair trade practices**

Key Words and Phrases

Commission

Contingent commission agreement

Review Questions

5-1. Distinguish between insurance agents and brokers in terms of the party each represents.

5-2. Summarize the steps that a candidate must take to obtain a state insurance agent's license.

5-3. Identify two key requirements an insurer must meet to be licensed by a state.

5-4. Provide three examples of reasons why some states require claims representatives to be licensed.

5-5. Identify what determines how an insurance agent receives sales commissions.

5-6. Why do insurers provide contingent commission agreements?

5-7. It is considered an unfair trade practice for insurance agents to make, issue, or
       circulate information that exhibits certain characteristics. Identify examples
       of such characteristics that indicate that information could be construed as
       misleading or as false advertising.

5-8. Describe the practice known as a tie-in sale.

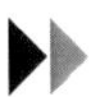

Answers to Assignment 4 Questions

NOTE: These answers are provided to give students a basic understanding of acceptable types of responses. They often are not the only valid answers and are not intended to provide an exhaustive response to the questions.

Educational Objective 1

1-1. Three factors that influence an agency relationship are legal roles, legal responsibilities, and scope of authority.

1-2. The two essential elements of an agency relationship are the agent's authority to act for the principal and the principal's control over the agent's actions on the principal's behalf.

1-3. The five duties that the laws of agency impose on insurance agents are these:

- Be loyal to the principal.

- Obey the principal's lawful instructions.

- Exercise a reasonable degree of care in actions on behalf of the principal. The agent must act as a reasonably prudent person would under the same or similar circumstances.

- Account promptly for any of the principal's money that the agent holds. Under the duty of accounting, the agent is responsible to the principal for all of the principal's money and property that comes into the agent's possession.

- Keep the principal informed of all facts relating to the agency relationship. This is the duty of relaying information.

1-4. Examples of the rights and duties that an agency contract addresses include the right to make insurance coverage effective and any limitations on that right. The contract also specifies how the agent is to handle funds, including stipulations on how and when the agent must remit premiums to the insurer. Insurance agency contracts usually give the agent the right to employ subagents, who may act on behalf of the insurer according to the terms of the agency contract.

1-5. The legal responsibilities of the principal to the agent include these:

- Pay the agent for services performed.

- Indemnify, or reimburse, the agent for any losses or damages suffered without the agent's fault, but arising out of the agent's actions on behalf of the principal. If a third party sues the agent in connection with activities performed on behalf of the principal, the principal must reimburse the agent for any liability incurred if the agent was not at fault.

1-6. Actual authority can be express authority or implied authority.

1-7. Alex can determine whether this type of arrangement is acceptable by consulting the agency contract or agency agreement. It specifies the scope of the agent's authority and relationship with the insurer.

Educational Objective 2

2-1. The three main insurance distribution systems are the independent agency and brokerage marketing system, the exclusive agency marketing system, and the direct writer marketing system.

2-2. An agency's most valuable asset is the ownership of its expiration lists.

2-3. Compensation for independent agents and brokers may be a flat percentage commission on all new and renewal business submitted or a contingent or profit-sharing commission based on volume or loss ratio goals.

2-4. The exclusive agency insurer handles many administrative functions for the exclusive agent, including policy issuance, premium collection, and claims processing.

2-5. Direct writer insurers can encourage their sales agents to develop new business by relieving producers of nonselling activities and compensating at a lower renewal rate.

2-6. Insurance portals benefit customers by offering the products and services of many insurance providers on one website. Although the leads that portals generate must subsequently be screened and fully underwritten by the insurers accepting the coverage, they can increase an insurer's market share and brand awareness.

2-7. An advantage of direct response is that commission costs, if any, are greatly reduced. However, a disadvantage is that advertising costs are typically higher.

2-8. Affinity marketing entails insurers targeting various customer groups based on profession, interests, hobbies, or attitudes.

2-9. Trade association advertising programs are intended to create a favorable image of association members as a group and to make the public familiar with the logos and other association symbols.

2-10. Insurers view financial institutions as beneficial strategic partners because they have a strong customer base, a predisposition to cross-selling, and strength at processing transactions. Financial institutions also efficiently use technology for database mining geared to specific products and services.

2-11. A mixed-marketing system requires consideration of these issues: maintaining consistent customer communications, providing a consistent customer experience, and matching the type of insurance with an appropriate distribution system and channel.

Educational Objective 3

3-1. Prospective clients can be located using several methods:

- Referrals from present clients
- Referrals from strategic partners, such as financial institutions and real estate brokers
- Advertising in multimedia and direct mail
- Interactive websites
- Telephone solicitations
- Cold canvass

3-2. Loss runs include, at a minimum, lists of losses and their total cost. More comprehensive loss runs provide details that can lead to additional questions and suggest areas of risk management improvement.

3-3. Businesses that are agency billed commonly use these three methods of transmitting premiums to insurers:

- Item basis—The premium (less commission) is forwarded to the insurer when the producer collects it or when it becomes due. The producer is usually not required to pay the insurer until the premium has been collected.

- Statement basis—The insurer sends a statement to the producer showing the premiums that are due. The producer is obligated to pay the premiums indicated as due or to show that the statement is in error.

- Account current basis—The producer periodically prepares a statement showing the premiums due to the insurer, after deducting appropriate commissions, and transmits that amount to the insurer. The producer must pay the insurer when the premium is due, as specified in the agency contract, even if the policyholders have not paid the producer.

3-4. Claims handling by qualified producers offers two major advantages: quicker service to policyholders and lower loss adjustment expenses to the insurer.

Educational Objective 4

4-1. An insurer must evaluate these factors relating to its profile when selecting distribution systems and channels:

- Its strategies and goals

- Its strengths

- Its existing and target markets

- Its geographic location

- Its desired or required degree of control over producers

4-2. Determining where its strengths lie, an insurer selects distribution systems and channels that maximize its opportunities to capture market share and minimize its weaknesses.

4-3. The insurer should consider the characteristics of its existing book of business. If agents or brokers own the expirations for current accounts, the insurer must either give up that business and start over or purchase the expirations from producers. Either option might be expensive, depending on the quality of the existing business. The insurer should also consider the possibility that a change in distribution systems and channels could disrupt communication channels, causing changes in communication patterns that can result in policyholder dissatisfaction and lost accounts.

Educational Objective 5

5-1. Generally, insurance agents are defined legally as representatives of the insurer(s) for which they sell insurance. Brokers are representatives of the insurance purchaser rather than of the insurer.

5-2. To obtain a state insurance agent's license, a candidate generally must pass an examination on insurance principles, insurance coverages, and insurance laws and regulations. Some states require candidates to accumulate a minimum number of hours of classroom study before taking this examination. In some states, completing a recognized professional designation program allows the candidate to waive the classroom and examination requirements.

5-3. By issuing a license to an insurer, a state indicates that the insurer meets minimum standards of financial strength, competence, and integrity and that it has complied with the state's insurance laws and is authorized to write certain types of insurance.

5-4. Some states require claims representatives to be licensed so that those who make claims decisions for insurers are aware of prohibited claims practices, have a minimum level of technical knowledge and skill, and understand how to handle insureds' claims fairly.

5-5. For insurance agents, the method of premium collection determines how sales commissions are received. If the insurer handles billings and collections (direct billing), the insurer periodically mails a commission check to the agency. If the agency collects the premiums (agency billing or producer billing), it subtracts its commission on each policy and remits the balance of collected premiums to the insurer.

5-6. Insurers sometimes provide contingent commission agreements as a form of incentive compensation for producers who exceed established benchmarks for profitability and volume of business.

5-7. It is an unfair trade practice for insurance agents or other insurance personnel to make, issue, or circulate information that exhibits any of these characteristics:

- Misrepresents the benefits, advantages, conditions, or terms of any insurance policy

- Misrepresents the dividends to be received on any insurance policy

- Makes false or misleading statements about dividends previously paid on any insurance policy

- Uses a name or title on insurance policies that misrepresents the true nature of the policies

5-8. A tie-in sale occurs when a producer requires that the purchase of insurance be "tied" to some other sale or financial arrangement.

Direct Your Learning 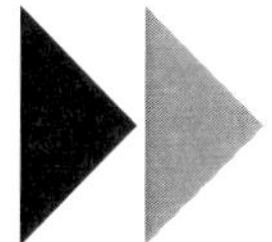

5

Underwriting and Ratemaking

Educational Objectives

After learning the content of this assignment, you should be able to:

1. Describe the purpose of underwriting.

2. Describe the underwriting activities typically performed by line and staff underwriters.

3. Describe the steps in the underwriting process.

4. Given the insurance rate and exposure units for a particular insurance policy, calculate the policy premium.

5. Describe the responsibilities of underwriting management.

6. Explain how individual states in the United States regulate underwriting activities through restrictions on unfair discrimination, cancellation, and nonrenewal.

7. Explain how insurance rates are developed.

Outline

▶ **Purpose of Underwriting**
  A. Guarding Against Adverse Selection
  B. Ensuring Adequate Policyholders' Surplus
  C. Enforcing Underwriting Guidelines

▶ **Underwriting Activities**
  A. Line Underwriting Activities
    1. Select Insureds
    2. Classify and Price Accounts
    3. Recommend or Provide Coverage
    4. Manage a Book of Business
    5. Support Producers and Customers
    6. Coordinate With Marketing Efforts
  B. Staff Underwriting Activities
    1. Research the Market
    2. Formulate Underwriting Policy
    3. Revise Underwriting Guidelines
    4. Evaluate Loss Experience
    5. Research and Develop Coverage Forms
    6. Review and Revise Pricing Plans
    7. Arrange Treaty Reinsurance
    8. Assist Others With Complex Accounts
    9. Conduct Underwriting Audits
    10. Participate in Industry Associations
    11. Conduct Education and Training

▶ **The Underwriting Process**
  A. Evaluate the Submission
    1. Weigh the Need for Information
    2. Gather the Necessary Information
  B. Develop Underwriting Alternatives
  C. Select an Underwriting Alternative
  D. Determine an Appropriate Premium
  E. Implement the Underwriting Decision
  F. Monitor the Underwriting Decision
    1. Monitor Individual Policies
    2. Monitor Books of Business

▶ **Premium Determination**
  A. Insurance Rates
  B. Exposure Units

C. Calculation of Premium (Rate x Exposure Units)
D. Other Factors Affecting Premium Determination

▶ **Underwriting Management**
  A. Participating in Insurer Management
  B. Arranging Reinsurance
  C. Delegating Underwriting Authority
  D. Developing and Enforcing Underwriting Guidelines
  E. Monitoring Underwriting Results

▶ **Regulation of Underwriting Activities**
  A. Prohibition of Unfair Discrimination
  B. Restrictions on Cancellation and Nonrenewal

▶ **Ratemaking**
  A. Insurance Advisory Organizations
  B. Insurance Rating Systems
    1. Loss Costs
    2. Class Rating
    3. Individual Rating
    4. Final Rate and Premium Determination

The SMART Online Practice Exams can be tailored to cover specific assignments, so you can focus your studies on topics you want to master.

For each assignment, you should define or describe each of the Key Words and Phrases and answer each of the Review and Application Questions.

Educational Objective 1
Describe the purpose of underwriting.

Key Words and Phrases

Book of business

Adverse selection

Capacity

Underwriting guidelines (underwriting guide)

Underwriting authority

Review Questions

1-1. Describe the approaches underwriters take to minimize the effects of adverse selection.

1-2. Describe the approaches underwriters take to ensure the adequacy of policy-
holders' surplus.

1-3. Describe the approaches underwriters take to ensure that the policies of
accepted applicants adhere to underwriting guidelines.

Educational Objective 2

Describe the underwriting activities typically performed by line and staff underwriters.

Key Words and Phrases

Line underwriter

Staff underwriter

Underwriting policy (underwriting philosophy)

Advisory organization

Prospective loss costs

Loss development

Trending

Treaty reinsurance

Facultative reinsurance

Underwriting audit

Review Questions

2-1. Describe the goals of effective account selection by line underwriters.

2-2. Describe the line underwriter responsibility of account classification.

2-3. How do line underwriters respond to requests from producers and applicants who want to know how coverage will respond to a particular type of loss?

2-4. Identify examples of goals for a book of business that a line underwriter works to help achieve.

2-5. Explain why line underwriters have an active interest in ensuring that producers' and insureds' needs are met.

2-6. Provide examples of items for which staff underwriters engage in ongoing research to evaluate.

2-7. Identify examples of items that may be included in underwriting guidelines.

2-8. When evaluating an insurer's loss experience, what products do staff underwriters usually target for analysis?

2-9. Explain how staff underwriters are involved in the development of coverage forms.

2-10. Identify factors that influence staff underwriters to update rates and rating plans.

2-11. Identify items on which underwriting audits focus.

Educational Objective 3
Describe the steps in the underwriting process.

Key Words and Phrases

Expert systems, or knowledge-based systems

Hazard

Physical hazard

Moral hazard

Morale hazard (attitudinal hazard)

Legal hazard

Information efficiency

Predictive analytics

Predictive modeling

Catastrophe model

Counteroffer

Experience rating

Schedule rating

Retrospective rating

Mix of business

Binder

Certificate of insurance

Review Questions

3-1. What are the steps in the underwriting process?

3-2. List five principal sources of underwriting information.

3-3. What are the four major ways an underwriter can modify a submission?

3-4. What factors, beyond the content of a submission itself, must an underwriter consider before selecting an underwriting alternative?

3-5. On what are insurance loss costs typically based?

3-6. Identify examples of events that trigger the monitoring of existing policies.

Educational Objective 4

Given the insurance rate and exposure units for a particular insurance policy, calculate the policy premium.

Key Words and Phrases

Rate

Rate manual

Exposure unit (unit of exposure)

Review Questions

4-1. Describe how underwriters use the Insurance Services Office, Inc. (ISO) *Commercial Lines Manual* (CLM) to determine premiums.

4-2. Describe the use of exposure units in insurance rating.

4-3. Provide two examples of exposure units.

4-4. Explain how to calculate a commercial insurance premium using the rate and exposure unit.

4-5. Why might an underwriter vary from the manual rate when determining premium?

4-6. What is the purpose of schedule rating plans?

Application Questions

4-7. A movie theater is applying for commercial general liability insurance. The rate is $100 per 1,000 admissions. The insurer estimates that the theater will have 50,000 admissions in the new policy period. Calculate the premium.

4-8. XYZ Company is applying for building insurance. The rate is $0.50 per $100 of building insurance. XYZ would like to insure the building for $500,000. Calculate the premium that XYZ would pay.

Educational Objective 5
Describe the responsibilities of underwriting management.

Review Questions

5-1. Identify the responsibilities underwriting management entails.

5-2. Provide examples of the kinds of decisions made at an insurer's senior-management level.

5-3. What is the distinction between treaty reinsurance and facultative reinsurance?

5-4. Identify the primary factors that influence the authority given to an underwriter.

5-5. Identify the elements listed in underwriting guidelines.

5-6. What is the purpose of constant monitoring of underwriting results?

Educational Objective 6

Explain how individual states in the United States regulate underwriting activities through restrictions on unfair discrimination, cancellation, and nonrenewal.

Review Questions

6-1. What is the difference between fair discrimination and unfair discrimination in insurance underwriting?

6-2. List three examples of unfair discrimination.

6-3. Identify the purpose of a market conduct evaluation.

6-4. Identify the purpose of requiring an insurer to provide notification to the insured of cancellation or nonrenewal within a specified period.

Application Question

6-5. An insurer has experienced excessive theft, vandalism, and suspicious fire losses in one territory. Upon investigation, the underwriters discovered that the major employer in the territory had closed. The resulting unemployment has created financial pressures on many former workers. It is suspected that the losses are a result of these pressures. The insurer has implemented a significant rate increase for all property in this territory as a result of the losses. Judge whether the rate increase implemented by the insurer is an example of fair or unfair discrimination.

Educational Objective 7
Explain how insurance rates are developed.

Key Words and Phrases

Ratemaking

Actuary

Loss costs

Insurance advisory organization

Law of large numbers

Contingencies

Class rating

Individual rate, or specific rate

Judgment rating

Final rate

Review Questions

7-1. Describe the role of insurance advisory organizations in ratemaking.

7-2. Explain why insurers often adjust data on historical loss costs in the ratemaking process.

7-3. What is the basic premise of an insurance classification and rating system?

Application Question

7-4. Interstate Trucking Company (ITC) has sixty employees. Among them are forty truck drivers who spend 95 percent of their time on the road. The organization also has seven customer service representatives who handle telephone calls and schedule shipments from the home office. Under ITC's workers compensation insurance, which group of employees would the company pay more to insure? Explain.

Answers to Assignment 5 Questions

NOTE: These answers are provided to give students a basic understanding of acceptable types of responses. They often are not the only valid answers and are not intended to provide an exhaustive response to the questions.

Educational Objective 1

1-1. To minimize the effects of adverse selection, underwriters carefully select the applicants whose loss exposures they are willing to insure, charge premiums that accurately reflect the loss exposures for those applicants they select, and monitor applications and books of business for unusual patterns of policy growth or loss.

1-2. Underwriters ensure the adequacy of policyholders' surplus by adhering to underwriting guidelines, making certain that all loss exposures are correctly identified, and charging adequate premiums for the applications that are accepted.

1-3. If loss exposures, risks, or policy limits on an application exceed an underwriter's authority, he or she will seek approval through supervisory and management ranks within the underwriting department.

Educational Objective 2

2-1. Effective account selection by line underwriters is essential to attaining these goals:

- Avoiding adverse selection

- Charging adequate premiums for accounts with a higher-than-average chance of loss

- Selecting better-than-average accounts for which the premium charged will be more than adequate

- Rationing an insurer's available capacity to obtain an optimum spread of loss exposures by location, class, size of risk, and line of business

2-2. Line underwriters are responsible for account classification, which is the process of grouping accounts with similar attributes so that they can be priced appropriately.

2-3. Line underwriters respond to requests from producers and applicants who want to know how coverage will respond to a particular type of loss by explaining the types of losses the coverage forms are designed to cover and the endorsements that must be added to provide the coverage desired.

2-4. The line underwriter works to ensure that each book of business achieves established goals, such as product mix, loss ratio, and written premium.

2-5. Line underwriters have an active interest in ensuring that producers' and insureds' needs are met because customer service activities and underwriting are often interwoven.

2-6. Items for which staff underwriters engage in ongoing research to evaluate include these:

- Effect of adding or deleting entire lines of business
- Effect of expanding into additional states or retiring from states presently serviced
- Optimal product mix in the book of business
- Premium volume goals

2-7. Some underwriting guidelines include systematic instructions for handling particular classes of commercial accounts. Such guidelines may identify specific hazards to evaluate, alternatives to consider, criteria to use when making the final decision, ways to implement the decision, and methods to monitor the decision. The guidelines may also provide pricing instructions and reinsurance-related information.

2-8. When evaluating an insurer's loss experience, staff underwriters usually target for analysis insurance products that have losses greater than those anticipated.

2-9. Staff underwriters work cooperatively with the actuarial and legal departments to develop new coverage forms and to modify existing coverage forms (those developed by advisory organizations or the insurer).

2-10. Staff underwriters review and update rates and rating plans continually, subject to regulatory constraints, to respond to changes in loss experience, competition, and inflation.

2-11. Underwriting audits focus on proper documentation, adherence to procedure and classification and rating practices, and conformity of selection decisions to the underwriting guide and bulletins.

Educational Objective 3

3-1. The underwriting process entails six steps:

- Evaluate the submission
- Develop underwriting alternatives
- Select an underwriting alternative
- Determine an appropriate premium
- Implement the underwriting decision
- Monitor the underwriting decision

3-2. Any of these are principal sources of underwriting information: producers, insurance applications, inspection reports, government records, financial rating services, loss data, field marketing personnel, premium auditors, and claim files.

3-3. An underwriter may modify a submission in these ways:

- Require risk control measures
- Change insurance rates, rating plans, or policy limits
- Amend policy terms and conditions
- Use facultative reinsurance

3-4. The underwriter must consider these factors before selecting an alternative:

- Underwriting authority

- Supporting business

- Mix of business

- Producer relationships

- Regulatory restrictions

3-5. Insurance loss costs are typically based on an elaborate classification system in which similar loss exposures are combined into the same rating classification.

3-6. The monitoring of existing policies usually occurs in response to any of these triggering events:

- Substantive policy changes

- Significant and unique losses

- Preparation for renewal

- Risk control and safety inspections

- Premium audits

Educational Objective 4

4-1. The ISO *CLM* provides classification tables that contain hundreds of classifications of commercial business operations. When calculating the premium for commercial accounts, underwriters typically determine the insured's business operation and then find the appropriate rating classification in the applicable classification table.

4-2. The fundamental measures of the loss exposures used in insurance rating are referred to as exposure units. Insurers use standardized exposure units for rating most types of insurance.

4-3. Examples of exposure units include these:

- Auto—each vehicle

- Commercial property—each $100 of insured value

- General liability—each $1,000 of gross sales (for example, a restaurant or retail store); each 1,000 of square feet of area (for example, a school); each $1,000 of payroll (for example, a consulting firm); each 1,000 admissions (for example, a movie theater)

- Homeowners—each $1,000 of insured value

- Workers compensation—each $100 of payroll

4-4. The number of exposure units is multiplied by the insurance rate.

4-5. Underwriters vary from the manual rate to reflect the reality of actual exposures to loss, the specific characteristics of those exposures, and competitive market influences.

4-6. Underwriters use schedule rating plans to reflect the differences between the applicant and the average risk. Underwriters apply scheduled rating credits to "better-than-average" risks and scheduled debits to "worse-than-average" risks.

4-7. The premium for the movie theater can be calculated in this way:

$$\text{Admissions} \div \text{unit size} = \text{Number of exposure units}$$
$$50{,}000 \text{ admissions} \div 1{,}000 \text{ admissions} = 50 \text{ exposure units}$$
$$\text{Rate per unit} \times \text{Number of exposure units} = \text{Premium}$$
$$\$100 \times 50 = \$5{,}000$$

4-8. The premium that XYZ Company would pay can be calculated in this way:

$$\text{Insured value} \div \text{Unit size} = \text{Number of exposure units}$$
$$\$500{,}000 \div \$100 = 5{,}000 \text{ units}$$
$$\text{Rate per unit} \times \text{Number of exposure units} = \text{Premium}$$
$$\$0.50 \times 5{,}000 = \$2{,}500$$

Educational Objective 5

5-1. The responsibilities of an insurer's underwriting management include these:

- Participating in the insurer's overall management

- Arranging reinsurance

- Delegating underwriting authority

- Developing and enforcing underwriting guidelines

- Monitoring underwriting results

5-2. Decisions made at an insurer's senior-management level might determine what type of marketing system the insurer uses, office locations, the emphasis that will be placed on personal and commercial insurance, and so forth.

5-3. The distinction between treaty reinsurance and facultative reinsurance is that treaty reinsurance automatically reinsures all eligible policies, while facultative reinsurance involves a separate transaction for each reinsured policy.

5-4. The authority given to an underwriter usually reflects the underwriter's experience and responsibilities and the types of insurance handled.

5-5. Underwriting guidelines list the factors that should be considered by the underwriter for each type of insurance, the desirable and undesirable characteristics of applicants relative to those factors, and the insurer's overall attitude toward applicants that exhibit those characteristics.

5-6. Constant monitoring of underwriting results enables underwriting management to adjust underwriting guidelines to accommodate changing conditions, goals, and results.

Educational Objective 6

6-1. Insurance underwriting strives for fair discrimination by applying the same standard or method of treatment to insureds—distinguishing among properties, businesses, and people; grouping them into categories; and charging a premium commensurate with their loss exposures. Unfair discrimination involves applying different standards or methods of treatment to insureds who have the same basic characteristics and loss potential.

6-2. Three examples of unfair discrimination include refusing to issue, cancel, or nonrenew coverage for an applicant or an insured solely on the basis of the applicant's or insured's geographic location (sometimes known as "redlining"), gender or marital status, or race.

6-3. Market conduct examinations are a process of evaluation used by state insurance departments to determine that an insurer's practices and procedures are in compliance with state laws and regulations and to help ensure equitable treatment of insureds and claimants.

6-4. Most states require that an insurer provide notification to the insured within a specified period, such as thirty days, before a policy is to be canceled or nonrenewed. This notice is intended to give the insured an opportunity to replace the coverage.

6-5. Although not all of the insurer's property policyholders in the territory would view it as fair, the action by the insurer is an example of fair discrimination. The premium increase being charged is commensurate with the increased loss exposures experienced by the property owners in the territory.

Educational Objective 7

7-1. Insurance advisory organizations help develop insurance rating systems by collecting reliable loss data that insurers use in establishing their rates and premiums. The organizations analyze the loss data collected to determine the average loss costs per exposure unit used in class rating.

7-2. Insurers often adjust data on historical loss costs in anticipation of losses that can be expected in the future as a result of inflation or other measurable trends. The resulting prospective loss costs indicate the amount of money an insurer can expect to pay for future claims for each exposure unit.

7-3. The basic premise of an insurance classification and rating system is that insureds with similar characteristics have similar potential loss frequency and severity. Even though wide variation in actual losses may occur from one insured to the next, aggregate losses among all members of the class should be predictably different from the losses of all members of another class who have different characteristics.

7-4. ITC would pay more for workers compensation insurance covering its truck drivers, based on the higher number of loss exposure units for the truck drivers' class rating. Long hours spent driving expose truck drivers to more traffic accidents than customer service representatives. As a class, truck drivers suffer more frequent and more severe injuries and disabilities. The rating class for truck drivers reflects this significantly higher loss exposure. The employer pays a higher rate for the higher loss exposure.

Direct Your Learning 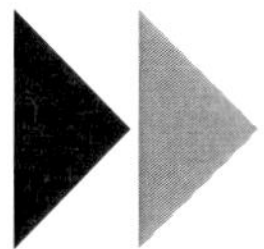

6

Claims

After learning the content of this assignment, you should be able to:

1. Explain how an insurer's claims function achieves each of its primary goals:
   - Keeping the insurer's promise
   - Supporting the insurer's profit goal
2. Describe claims departments in terms of the following:
   - How they can be structured
   - The types and functions of claims personnel
   - How their performance can be measured
3. Describe the activities in the claims handling process.
4. Explain how claims representatives handle these aspects of property insurance claims:
   - Verifying coverage
   - Determining the amount of loss
   - Concluding the claim and exercising subrogation and salvage rights
5. Explain how claims representatives handle these aspects of liability insurance claims:
   - Verifying coverage
   - Determining the cause of loss
   - Determining the amount of damages
   - Concluding the claim
6. Identify the special considerations for property catastrophe claims.

6

7. Describe the elements of good-faith claims handling and the practices prohibited by unfair claims practices laws.

Outline

▶ **Goals of the Claims Function**
  A. Keeping the Insurer's Promise
  B. Supporting the Insurer's Profit Goal
▶ **Claims Department Structure, Personnel, and Performance**
  A. Claims Department Structure
  B. Claims Personnel
    1. Staff Claims Representatives
    2. Independent Adjusters
    3. Third-Party Administrators
    4. Producers
    5. Public Adjusters
  C. Claims Performance Measures
    1. Profitability Measures
    2. Quality Measures
▶ **The Claims Handling Process**
  A. Acknowledging and Assigning the Claim
  B. Identifying the Policy and Setting Reserves
    1. Identifying the Policy
    2. Setting Reserves
  C. Contacting the Insured or the Insured's Representative
  D. Investigating the Claim
  E. Documenting the Claim
  F. Determining the Cause of Loss, Liability, and the Loss Amount
  G. Concluding the Claim
    1. Payments
    2. Claim Denial
    3. Alternative Dispute Resolution and Litigation
    4. Closing Reports
▶ **Aspects of Property Insurance Claims**
  A. Verifying Coverage
  B. Determining the Amount of Loss
    1. Common Valuation Methods
    2. Valuation Process

  C. Concluding the Claim
    1. Subrogation
    2. Salvage Rights
▶ **Aspects of Liability Insurance Claims**
  A. How Liability Claims Differ From Property Claims
  B. Verifying Coverage
  C. Determining the Cause of Loss
  D. Determining the Amount of Damages
    1. Compensatory Damages
    2. Punitive Damages
  E. Concluding the Claim
▶ **Special Considerations for Property Catastrophe Claims**
▶ **Good-Faith Claims Handling**
  A. Law of Bad Faith
  B. Elements of Good-Faith Claims Handling
    1. Thorough, Timely, and Unbiased Investigation
    2. Complete and Accurate Documentation
    3. Fair Evaluation
    4. Good-Faith Negotiation
    5. Regular and Prompt Communication
    6. Competent Legal Advice
    7. Effective Claims Management
  C. Unfair Claims Practices Laws

When you take the randomized full practice exams in the SMART Online Practice Exams product, you are seeing the same kinds of questions you will see when you take the actual exam.

For each assignment, you should define or describe each of the Key Words and Phrases and answer each of the Review and Application Questions.

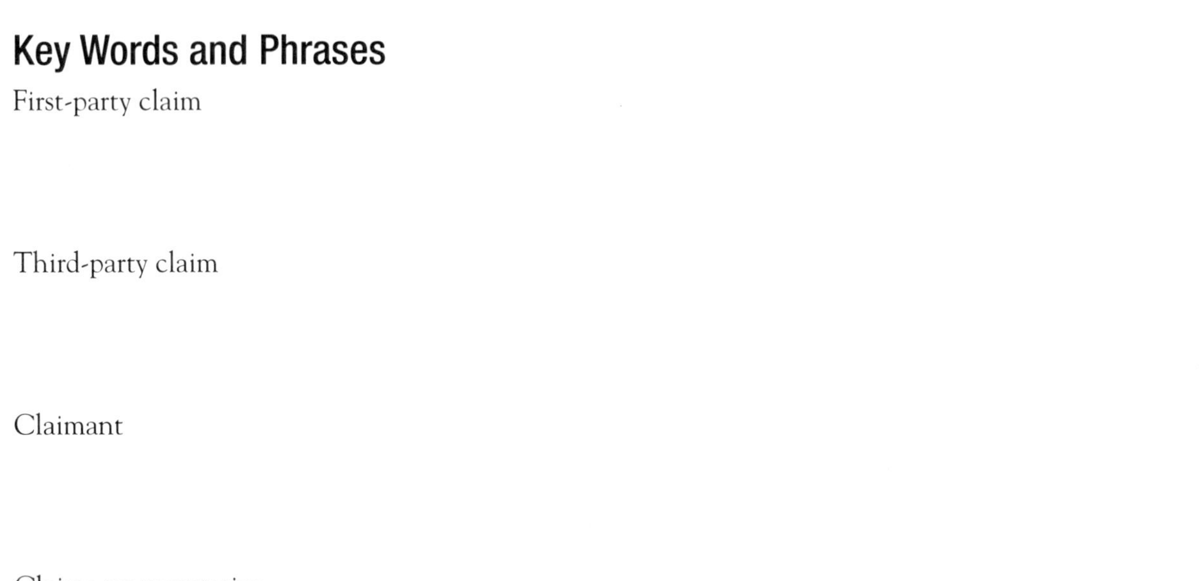

Educational Objective 1

Explain how an insurer's claims function achieves each of its primary goals:

- **Keeping the insurer's promise**
- **Supporting the insurer's profit goal**

Key Words and Phrases

First-party claim

Third-party claim

Claimant

Claims representative

Review Questions

1-1. What are the two primary goals of the claims function?

1-2. What contractual promise does an insurer fulfill, and how is it fulfilled?

1-3. In what ways do the following claims function personnel help the insurer generate an underwriting profit?

a.   Claims managers

b.   Claims staff

c.   Claims representatives

Application Question

1-4. Jason, a claims manager for Insurance Company, held a meeting of the claims representatives in his department. Jason asked the claims representatives to identify specific ways that they can help the company comply with its contractual promise and support its profit goals. From the viewpoint of a claims representative in this meeting, explain the claims representatives' roles in fulfilling these two goals of the claims function.

Educational Objective 2

Describe claims departments in terms of the following:

- **How they can be structured**
- **The types and functions of claims personnel**
- **How their performance can be measured**

Key Words and Phrases

Third-party administrator (TPA)

Independent adjuster

Public adjuster

Review Questions

2-1. Describe each of these claims personnel to distinguish each position from the others:

    a. Staff claims representatives

    b. Independent adjusters

    c. Third-party administrators

    d. Producers

    e. Public adjusters

2-2. Identify the two types of performance measures used to evaluate a claims department's performance.

Educational Objective 3
Describe the activities in the claims handling process.

Key Words and Phrases

Nonwaiver agreement

Reservation of rights letter

Subrogation

Mediation

Arbitration

Appraisal

Mini-trial

Summary jury trial

Review Questions

3-1. Identify the goal of assigning a claim.

3-2. If it is apparent from the loss notice that coverage may not be available for the loss, the claims representative should prepare either one of which two documents to notify the insured of this concern while still preserving the insurer's rights?

3-3. Explain why establishing and maintaining adequate reserves is important for an insurer's financial stability.

3-4. Explain why establishing reserves for liability claims can be difficult.

3-5. When an insurer pays a claim to an insured for a loss caused by a negligent third party, how can the insurer recover that payment amount from that negligent third party?

3-6. Identify three crucial parts of claims documentation.

3-7. What do claims representatives use to determine the cause of a loss?

3-8. Identify examples of alternative dispute resolution (ADR) techniques.

Educational Objective 4

Explain how claims representatives handle these aspects of property insurance claims:

- **Verifying coverage**
- **Determining the amount of loss**
- **Concluding the claim and exercising subrogation and salvage rights**

Key Words and Phrases

Insurable interest

Actual cash value (ACV)

Depreciation

Replacement cost

Agreed value method

Salvage rights

Constructive total loss

Review Questions

4-1. Identify the three crucial components of the claims handling process for property insurance claims.

4-2. What are the three steps involved in initial verification of coverage?

4-3. Identify the four questions for which the claims representative must seek answers to verify that a claim is covered.

4-4. When determining the amount of loss for a personal property claim, what is the most important information?

4-5. Identify the most common property valuation methods.

4-6. Identify the three factors that can be used to determine the replacement cost of real property.

4-7. Provide examples of factors that can complicate the negotiation phase of the property insurance claims process.

4-8. Describe the basic purpose of subrogation.

4-9. What are salvage rights?

Application Question

4-10. A covered cause of loss destroys a family's three-year-old television. The television would cost $800 to replace with a comparable (of like kind and quality) new television. A television is generally expected to be used for six years. Explain how the claims representative would determine the covered television's actual cash value (ACV).

Educational Objective 5

Explain how claims representatives handle these aspects of liability insurance claims:

- **Verifying coverage**
- **Determining the cause of loss**
- **Determining the amount of damages**
- **Concluding the claim**

Key Words and Phrases

Damages

Compensatory damages

Special damages

General damages

Punitive damages (exemplary damages)

Review Questions

5-1. Identify the four key aspects of claims handling for liability insurance claims.

5-2. Identify three reasons why liability claims adjusting differs from and may be more difficult than property claims adjusting.

5-3. Describe the process a claims representative follows to verify that a property claim is covered.

5-4. What are damages?

5-5. Identify the purpose of compensatory damages.

5-6. Identify the purpose of punitive damages.

Educational Objective 6

Identify the special considerations for property catastrophe claims.

Review Questions

6-1. Identify the purposes that detailed contingency plans for a catastrophe serve for an insurer.

6-2. Identify examples of possible insurer responses to increased employee stress levels in the aftermath of a catastrophe.

6-3. Provide examples of changes that insurers can make to their work operations to address catastrophes.

6-4. Identify examples of possible insurer responses to having insufficient claims staff to handle the volume of incoming claims associated with a catastrophe.

Educational Objective 7

Describe the elements of good-faith claims handling and the practices prohibited by unfair claims practices laws.

Review Questions

7-1. Explain why claims representatives' actions may be closely scrutinized and are often criticized.

7-2. Why do most bad-faith claims for breach of the implied duty of good faith and fair dealing arise under insurance-related contracts rather than other types of contracts?

7-3. Identify the elements of good-faith claims handling.

7-4. Identify the elements of a thorough claims investigation.

7-5. Explain why promptness is a crucial element of fair claims evaluation.

7-6. Identify how claims representatives should resolve disputes over settlement amounts.

7-7. Explain why communicating with all parties to a claim is a crucial aspect of good-faith claims handling and resolving claims.

7-8. When do insurance regulators usually learn of unfair claims practices?

Answers to Assignment 6 Questions

NOTE: These answers are provided to give students a basic understanding of acceptable types of responses. They often are not the only valid answers and are not intended to provide an exhaustive response to the questions.

Educational Objective 1

1-1. The two primary goals of the claims function are compliance with the contractual promise and support of the insurer's profit goal.

1-2. The contractual promise that the insurer fulfills, as set out in the insuring agreement, is to pay, defend, or indemnify the insured in the event of a covered loss. The insurer fulfills this promise by providing fair, prompt, and equitable service to the policyholder, either directly for first-party claims or indirectly for third-party claims.

1-3. These are ways in which the following claims function personnel help the insurer generate an underwriting profit:

   a. Claims managers help the insurer generate an underwriting profit by managing all claims function expenses, setting appropriate spending policies, and using appropriately priced providers and services.

   b. Claims staff can help the insurer generate an underwriting profit by avoiding overspending on costs of handling claims, claims operations, and other expenses.

   c. Claims representatives help the insurer generate an underwriting profit by working to settle claims fairly, thus reducing the possibility of costly litigation and regulatory oversight or penalties.

1-4. Claims representatives help the insurer fulfill its contractual promise by handling claims in a way that promotes peace of mind for the policyholder and that quickly restores a claimant to his or her pre-loss condition. Claims representatives, along with all claims staff, can support the insurer's profit goals by avoiding overspending on claims handling, operations, and other expenses. In addition, claims representatives can help the insurer avoid costly litigation, regulatory oversight, and penalties by treating policyholders and other claimants fairly to ensure satisfaction with the claims service.

Educational Objective 2

2-1. Claims personnel can be distinguished among one another in these ways:

   a. Staff claims representatives are employees of an insurer, and they handle most claims. They may include inside claims representatives, who handle claims exclusively from the insurer's office, and field claims representatives, who handle claims both inside and outside the office.

   b. Independent adjusters are claims representatives with whom insurers contract to handle claims in strategic locations, such as disaster sites; to meet desired service levels; or when special skills are needed.

c. Self-insured businesses can often contract with third-party administrators (TPAs), who handle claims, keep claims records, and perform statistical analyses. TPAs are often associated with large independent adjusting firms or with subsidiaries of insurance companies.

d. Producers can include agents, brokers, employees of insurers, or intermediaries. Insurers give some producers the authority to pay claims up to a certain amount. Those producers can issue claim payments, called drafts, directly to insureds for covered claims, thus reducing the time an insured waits for payment.

e. A public adjuster is an organization or a person hired by an insured to represent the insured in a claim in exchange for a fee. Generally, the public adjuster prepares the insured's claim and negotiates the settlement with the staff claims representative or independent adjuster.

2-2. The two types of performance measures used to evaluate a claims department's performance are profitability measures and quality measures.

Educational Objective 3

3-1. The goal is to assign the claim to a claims representative who possesses the appropriate skills to handle it.

3-2. The two documents that preserve the insurer's rights when coverage is doubtful are a nonwaiver agreement and a reservation of rights letter. The claims representative should prepare either one of the two documents in such a situation.

3-3. Establishing and maintaining adequate reserves is important for an insurer's financial stability because reserves affect the insurer's ability to maintain and increase business.

3-4. Establishing reserves for liability claims can be difficult because the eventual payment on a liability claim, which may not be made for several years after the claim is made, can vary significantly from the original reserve.

3-5. When an insurer pays a claim to an insured for a loss caused by a negligent third party, the insurer can recover that payment amount from the negligent third party through the right of subrogation.

3-6. Three crucial parts of the claims documentation are diary systems, file status notes, and file reports.

3-7. Claims representatives use the facts of the loss to determine the cause of the loss.

3-8. Examples of ADR techniques include mediation, arbitration, appraisals, mini-trials, and summary jury trials.

Educational Objective 4

4-1. The three crucial components of the claims handling process for property insurance claims are verifying coverage, determining the amount of loss, and concluding the claim and exercising subrogation and salvage rights.

4-2. The three steps involved in initial verification of coverage are these:

a. Confirming that a valid policy was in effect

b. Determining that the date of the loss falls within the policy period

c. Establishing whether the damaged property is insured under the policy

4-3.   The four questions for which the claims representative must seek answers to verify that a claim is covered are these:

- Does the insured have an insurable interest in the property?
- Is the damaged property covered by the policy?
- Is the cause of loss covered by the policy?
- Do any additional coverages, endorsements, or coverage limitations apply?

4-4.   For personal property, the most important information is what property was damaged or destroyed.

4-5.   The most common property valuation methods are actual cash value, replacement cost, and agreed value.

4-6.   The replacement cost of real property can be determined using these three factors:

- Square footage of the property
- Type and quality of construction
- Construction cost per square foot

4-7.   Factors that can complicate the negotiation phase of the property insurance claims process include a large number of damaged items, property of high value, or disagreement between the insured and the claims representative regarding the value or circumstances of the loss.

4-8.   The basic purpose of subrogation is to prevent an insured from collecting from both the insurer and the party at fault for the same loss.

4-9.   Salvage rights are the insurer's rights to recover and sell or otherwise dispose of insured property on which the insurer has paid a total loss or a constructive total loss.

4-10.   The claims representative must place a value on the television by determining the extent of depreciation that should be considered. Because a television might be used for six years and is now three years old, the claims representative estimates the depreciation from normal wear at 50 percent. Therefore, with a replacement cost of $800 and depreciation estimated at 50 percent, the ACV of the destroyed television is $400. A payment of $400 would indemnify the insured for the loss of the television.

Educational Objective 5

5-1.   The four key aspects of claims handling for liability insurance claims are verifying coverage, determining the cause of loss, determining the amount of damages, and concluding the claim.

5-2.   Liability claims adjusting differs from and may be more difficult than property claims adjusting for three reasons. First, the claimant is a third party who has been injured or whose property has been damaged by the insured. Second, a liability claim may involve bodily injury. Third, liability claim settlement sometimes involves a claim for damage that the insured has allegedly caused to the property of others.

5-3. The process a claims representative follows to verify that a property claim is covered includes establishing whether a valid policy was in effect and, if so, determining whether the date of the loss falls within the policy period and whether any additional coverages, endorsements, or coverage limitations apply. The claims representative must also determine whether the insured is legally responsible for the loss.

5-4. Damages are money claimed by, or a monetary award to, a party who has suffered bodily injury or property damage for which another party is legally responsible.

5-5. Compensatory damages are intended to compensate a victim for harm actually suffered. They include special damages and general damages.

5-6. The purpose of punitive damages is to punish the wrongdoer and to deter others from committing similar wrongs.

Educational Objective 6

6-1. Detailed contingency plans for a catastrophe serve these purposes for an insurer:

- Identifying weaknesses, bottlenecks, and potential difficulties

- Permitting staff to clearly understand their roles and responsibilities during a crisis in advance, so that they can react productively and not emotionally

- Keeping the organization free to focus on handling claims without reallocating essential resources to resolve problems for which it was unprepared

6-2. Examples of possible insurer responses to increased employee stress levels in the aftermath of a catastrophe include these:

- Train employees in stress management and have counselors available on site

- Provide temporary daycare services and meals as other businesses are closed and employees work longer hours

6-3. Examples of changes that insurers can make to their work operations to address catastrophes include these:

- Developing and using abbreviated claims handling procedures to speed processing

- Temporarily increasing claim settlement authority to producers for the duration of the catastrophe response

- Temporarily transferring claim settlement authority to preselected independent adjusting firms

- Bringing in catastrophe teams of claims representatives from other regions

- Making advance payments to policyholders for costs such as additional living expenses

- Immediately settling all questions of property valuation in favor of the policyholder

- Suspending all but the most essential recordkeeping

- Reallocating available employees in critical work areas

6-4. These are some examples of possible insurer responses to having insufficient claims staff to handle the volume of incoming claims associated with a catastrophe:

- Identify and train staff from other areas to assist

- Establish relationships with independent adjusters to help manage overflow

- Bring in catastrophe teams of claims representatives from other regions

Educational Objective 7

7-1. Claims representatives' actions may be closely scrutinized and are often criticized because interactions with claims representatives are often the only personal contacts that the general public has with an insurer.

7-2. Most bad-faith claims for breach of the implied duty of good faith and fair dealing arise under insurance-related contracts rather than other types of contracts because, in insurance contracts, the insurer not only dictates the terms of the contract (the policy), but also usually controls the claims investigation, evaluation, negotiation, and settlement and therefore has more "bargaining power" than the insured.

7-3. Good-faith claims handling consists of these elements:

- Thorough, timely, and unbiased investigation

- Complete and accurate documentation

- Fair evaluation

- Good-faith negotiation

- Regular and prompt communication

- Competent legal advice

- Effective claims management

7-4. For an investigation to be considered thorough, claims representatives should collect all relevant and necessary evidence, develop the information and documentation necessary to determine liability and damages, and make decisions when they believe they have sufficient information to do so. In a thorough investigation, the claims representative is alert for new information that may change the course of the claim.

7-5. Promptness is a crucial element of fair claims evaluation because compliance with statutory time limits for completion of evaluations of coverage and damages can help reduce the insurer's exposure to bad-faith claims. Promptness is also important in responding to the claimant, the insured, or their respective lawyers' demands. Promptness is particularly important when there is a demand for settlement that is at or near the policy limits.

7-6. To resolve disputes over settlement amounts, claims representatives should use policy provisions, such as arbitration clauses, when applicable.

7-7. Communicating with all parties to a claim is a crucial aspect of good-faith claims handling and resolving claims because they expect it, they are most likely to make a bad-faith claim, and they may have the most important information about an accident.

7-8. Insurance regulators usually learn of unfair claims practices when they receive complaints from insureds and claimants.

Direct Your Learning 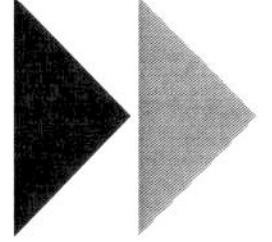

7

Risk Management

Educational Objectives

After learning the content of this assignment, you should be able to:

1. Describe the basic purpose and scope of risk management in terms of the following:

   - How risk management is practiced by individuals and organizations

   - The basic distinction between traditional risk management and enter-prise-wide risk management

2. Explain how to identify and analyze loss exposures.

3. Describe the risk management techniques for risk control and risk financing.

4. Explain how to select the appropriate risk management techniques, implement the selected techniques, and monitor a risk management program.

5. Explain how risk management benefits businesses, individuals, families, society, and insurers.

6. Applying the risk management process, recommend appropriate risk man-agement techniques for handling loss exposures of an individual, a family, or a business.

Outline

▶ **Basic Purpose and Scope of Risk Management**
  A. Risk Management for Individuals and Organizations
  B. Traditional Risk Management and Enterprise-Wide Risk Management

▶ **Identifying and Analyzing Loss Exposures**
  A. Identifying Loss Exposures
     1. Physical Inspection
     2. Loss Exposure Surveys
     3. Loss History Analysis
  B. Analyzing Loss Exposures
     1. Loss Frequency
     2. Loss Severity

▶ **Examining the Feasibility of Risk Management Techniques**
  A. Risk Control
     1. Avoidance
     2. Loss Prevention
     3. Loss Reduction
     4. Separation
     5. Duplication
  B. Risk Financing
     1. Retention
     2. Transfer

▶ **Selecting, Implementing, and Monitoring Risk Management Techniques**
  A. Selecting the Appropriate Risk Management Techniques
  B. Selection Based on Financial Criteria
  C. Selection Based on Informal Guidelines
  D. Implementing the Selected Risk Management Techniques
     1. Deciding What Should Be Done
     2. Deciding Who Should Be Responsible
     3. Communicating Risk Management Information
     4. Allocating Costs of the Risk Management Program
  E. Monitoring Results and Revising the Risk Management Program

▶ **Benefits of Risk Management**
  A. Benefits of Risk Management to Businesses
  B. Benefits of Risk Management to Individuals and Families
  C. Benefits of Risk Management to Society
  D. Benefits of Risk Management to Insurers

▶ **Applying the Risk Management Process**
  A. Tony and Maria
  B. Identifying and Analyzing Loss Exposures
  C. Examining, Selecting, and Implementing Risk Management Techniques
  D. Monitoring Results and Revising the Risk Management Program

Reward yourself after you reach specific goals.

For each assignment, you should define or describe each of the Key Words and Phrases and answer each of the Review and Application Questions.

Educational Objective 1

Describe the basic purpose and scope of risk management in terms of the following:

- **How risk management is practiced by individuals and organizations**
- **The basic distinction between traditional risk management and enterprise-wide risk management**

Key Words and Phrases

Pure risk

Speculative risk

Review Questions

1-1. Explain how risk management practices differ between individuals and organizations.

1-2. Describe the difference in scope between traditional risk management and enterprise-wide risk management.

1-3. Explain how the focus of risk management efforts differs for traditional risk management and enterprise-wide risk management.

Educational Objective 2
Explain how to identify and analyze loss exposures.

Review Questions

2-1. What are the three most commonly used tools for identifying loss exposures?

2-2. Identify what is examined in a physical inspection to identify the loss exposures for a business.

2-3. When deciding the proper treatment for a loss exposure, what action may be indicated if a particular type of loss occurs frequently or if its frequency has been increasing in recent years?

Application Question

2-4. Rachael, an entrepreneur, is beginning a risk management program for her small Internet consulting business. She rents office space and owns the computer equipment and diagnostic tools that she uses in her business. Rachael has identified her loss exposures and found that her business is subject to professional liability exposures. Because Rachael is educated and experienced in her business, her loss frequency should be minimal, but the potential loss severity from defending a significant claim could be financially crippling for Rachael's business. If bad publicity from such a claim resulted in similar actions, professional liability claims could destroy her business. Explain why Rachael should not retain her entire liability loss exposure.

Educational Objective 3

Describe the risk management techniques for risk control and risk financing.

Key Words and Phrases

Avoidance

Retention

Review Questions

3-1. In general, what is the goal of risk control techniques?

3-2. What are the two main objectives of an inspection report?

3-3. Give an example of each of these risk financing techniques.

a. Partial retention

b. Noninsurance risk transfer

Application Question

3-4. To handle the loss exposures of the apartment buildings she owns, Mandy has purchased apartment buildings in four different cities that are geographically spread throughout the state of Texas. She selected properties that were inland enough that they would not be affected by hurricane winds or flooding. She also purchased a property and liability insurance policy on the apartment buildings with a $2,000 deductible on each building. Identify the risk management techniques that Mandy has used to manage her apartment loss exposures.

Educational Objective 4

Explain how to select the appropriate risk management techniques, implement the selected techniques, and monitor a risk management program.

Review Questions

4-1. Identify and describe the two common methods for selecting risk management techniques.

4-2. To effectively implement a risk management program, what decisions must a risk manager make?

4-3. What is involved in monitoring and revising the risk management program?

Application Question

4-4. Raymond is the risk manager for Sansseam Industries, a million dollar direct marketing company for ladies clothing. Raymond has identified ten risk management techniques that he believes may be valuable for Sansseam's risk management program. Explain an appropriate method for Raymond to use in assessing the ten risk management techniques.

Educational Objective 5
Explain how risk management benefits businesses, individuals, families, society, and insurers.

Review Questions

5-1. How can a business benefit from risk management?

5-2. How can individuals and families benefit from risk management?

5-3. How does society as a whole benefit from risk management?

5-4. How do insurers benefit from risk management?

Application Question

5-5. Maria is the head of a family household. Her teenage son has just purchased his first vehicle and is questioning the value of purchasing insurance. He is complaining that it is too expensive and he can afford only minimum limits. How can Maria apply the benefits of risk management to individuals and families to encourage him to purchase adequate insurance coverage?

Educational Objective 6

Applying the risk management process, recommend appropriate risk management techniques for handling loss exposures of an individual, a family, or a business.

Application Questions

6-1. Donald is the sole proprietor of a small used auto sales business. He has no employees. In order to develop a risk management program, Donald identified and analyzed his business loss exposures and determined that he should purchase property and liability insurance. He also purchased coverage for business interruption. Donald selected a $100,000 deductible on his business property policy because he believed he could retain that amount of loss. Shortly after Donald purchased his insurance policies, the business sustained an $85,000 vandalism loss for damage to some of the inventory and the building. Donald paid for this loss, depleting most of his business savings account.

Donald has completed the first five steps in the risk management process. Explain how the vandalism loss would be considered in the last step in the risk management process.

6-2. Gayle owns a small independent insurance agency. The agency offers property and liability insurance coverages from four insurers to prospective and existing clients. Gayle rents office space from Tyler Property Management and owns her office furnishings and equipment, including three computers and two laser jet printers. Gayle's agency maintains investments totaling $1 million. Gayle pays two customer service representatives to meet with customers, complete and submit insurance applications, help handle insurance claims, and issue agency drafts. Gayle pays for continuing education for herself and her employees to enable them to maintain their agents' licenses in their state. Attending educational seminars sometimes involves business travel. Gayle has recognized the need for a risk management program.

a.   Identify the first two steps of the risk management process and apply them to the information provided on Gayle's agency.

b.   Evaluate each of these risk management techniques and explain how each could apply to Gayle's agency: avoidance, loss prevention or loss reduction, insurance, and retention.

6-3. Dave and Gloria have developed and implemented a risk management program for their household. They own their home and four autos. Each is the primary operator of one of the autos, and their teenage son and daughter each use one of the other vehicles. The couple owns a motor boat, and they enjoy taking their family, and sometimes friends, along when they take the boat to a nearby lake for recreation. The couple's risk management program includes property (real and personal) and liability insurance for their home, autos, and boat and a $1 million umbrella policy. They installed a security and fire alarm system for their home and pay a fee for related services. The couple also purchased life insurance policies on themselves and their children. To monitor and revise their risk management program, Dave and Gloria must consider any changes to their situation. For each event below, suggest a change to their risk management program and identify the risk management technique. Treat each event independently of the other.

a.   Dave and Gloria's sixteen-year-old son, Zach, has a hobby of rock climbing. Zach started rock climbing with a group of teenagers from his school. Because of his advanced experience, Zach often led the other teens in their excursions.

b. Dave was advised that his job was being downsized. He eventually found another job, but he accepted a significant pay cut. The couple found that they could not afford to pay the insurance that they paid in the past, but they love their home and need four autos for their family.

Answers to Assignment 7 Questions

NOTE: These answers are provided to give students a basic understanding of acceptable types of responses. They often are not the only valid answers and are not intended to provide an exhaustive response to the questions.

Educational Objective 1

1-1. Individuals and families often practice risk management informally (purchasing insurance policies and contributing to savings plans) without explicitly following a risk management process. In smaller organizations, risk management is not usually a dedicated function, but one of many tasks carried out by the owner or senior manager. In many larger organizations, the risk management function is conducted as part of a formalized risk management program.

1-2. The scope of traditional risk management is on losses generated by pure, as opposed to speculative, risks.

The scope of enterprise-wide risk management encompasses all types of risk with the intent of maximizing the organization's value.

1-3. Traditional risk management focuses on managing safety, purchasing insurance, and controlling financial recovery from losses generated by hazard risk. Enterprise-wide risk management focuses on managing all of the organization's key risks and opportunities with the intent of maximizing the organization's value.

Educational Objective 2

2-1. The three most commonly used tools for identifying loss exposures are physical inspections of the premises, loss exposure surveys, and loss history analyses.

2-2. During a physical inspection to identify the loss exposures of a business, a risk manager should inspect all locations, operations, maintenance routines, safety practices, work processes, and other activities in which the organization is involved.

2-3. If a particular type of loss occurs frequently, or if its frequency has been increasing in recent years, the risk manager may decide that procedures for controlling the risk are necessary.

2-4. Rachael should not retain her entire professional liability loss exposure because even though the loss frequency for this loss exposure is expected to be low, the probable loss severity is high and difficult to calculate.

Educational Objective 3

3-1. Risk control techniques attempt to decrease the frequency and/or severity of losses or make them more predictable.

3-2. These are the two main objectives of an inspection report:

- To provide a thorough description of the applicant's operation so that the underwriter can make an accurate assessment when deciding whether to accept the application for insurance

- To provide an evaluation of the applicant's current risk control measures and recommend improvements in risk control efforts

3-3. These are some possible examples of risk financing techniques:

    a. When an insured purchases insurance with a deductible and an insured loss occurs, the deductible results in a partial retention (the deductible amount) of the insured's loss exposure.

    b. A hold-harmless provision included in a lease that enables the landlord to transfer the financial consequences of a liability exposure arising out of the tenant's activities is a noninsurance risk transfer technique. In this case, the hold-harmless agreement might state that the tenant agrees to indemnify the landlord for any damages the landlord becomes legally obligated to pay because of injury or damage occurring on the premises occupied by the tenant.

3-4. Mandy used these techniques to manage her apartment loss exposures:

- Mandy's purchase of apartment buildings that are geographically spread is a separation technique.

- Mandy's selection of properties that are inland to avoid hurricane winds and flooding is an avoidance technique.

- Mandy's purchase of insurance on the apartment buildings is a transfer technique.

- Mandy's selection of a $2,000 deductible on each building applies a retention technique for that portion of the loss exposure.

Educational Objective 4

4-1. These are two common methods for selecting risk management techniques:

- Financial criteria—By forecasting how selection of a particular risk management technique will affect profits or output, an organization can choose the risk management technique that is likely to be the most financially beneficial.

- Informal guidelines—Some guidelines include not retaining more than you can afford to lose, not retaining large exposures to save a little premium, not spending a lot of money for a little protection, and not considering insurance a substitute for risk control.

4-2. The risk manager must decide what should be done to implement the program, who should be responsible for implementing the program (management or the risk manager), how the program and any needed modifications should be communicated, and how the costs of the program should be allocated.

4-3. To monitor and modify the risk management program, the risk manager must periodically identify and analyze new and existing loss exposures and then reexamine, select, and implement appropriate risk management techniques, restarting the risk management process. Monitoring the program ranges from handling routine matters to making complex decisions concerning new activities to initiate or avoid.

4-4. Raymond should consider Sansseam's objectives for increasing profits and/or operating efficiency. He should forecast how each of the ten techniques will affect profits or output and choose those techniques that are likely to be the most financially beneficial in meeting Sansseam's objectives.

Educational Objective 5

5-1. A business can benefit from risk management in the following ways:

- Improved access to affordable insurance

- Increased opportunities for the insured

- Achievement of business goals through better management of loss exposures

5-2. Individuals and families can benefit from risk management in the following ways:

- Ability to cope more effectively with financial disasters

- Greater peace of mind because loss exposures are under control

- Reduction in expenses by handling loss exposures in the most economical fashion

- Ability to continue activities following an accident or other loss

- Incentive to take more chances and make more aggressive decisions

5-3. Society as a whole benefits from risk management in the following ways:

- Reduction in the number of persons dependent on society for support

- Fewer disruptions in the economic and social environment

- Stimulation of economic growth

5-4. Insurers benefit from risk management in the following ways:

- Risk management creates a positive effect on an insurer's underwriting results, loss ratio, and overall profitability.

- Risk management provides more knowledgeable consumers of insurance.

- Risk management stimulates insurers to create innovative products and maintain competitive prices and services.

5-5. These benefits could encourage Maria's son to purchase adequate insurance coverage:

- Coping with financial disasters—"If you cause an accident, the insurance will pay for the damage to the other vehicles and for the injuries to the other passengers. Otherwise, they may sue you personally and it could disrupt your standard of living."

- Enjoying greater peace of mind—"With insurance, you can be sure that your loss exposures are under control and handled cost-effectively."

- Continuing activities following an accident—"If you purchase insurance to cover your car, you will be able to repair this vehicle or buy another one if this one is damaged in an accident."

Educational Objective 6

6-1.   The last step in the risk management process is monitoring results and revising the risk management program. In completing this step, Donald's vandalism loss experience indicates that Donald overlooked the need for loss prevention or reduction techniques. He may need to implement some techniques, such as installing a tall fence around his auto lot and contracting with a security company to help prevent losses. He might also consider reducing his property deductible. Donald has to restart the risk management process based on his experiences.

6-2.   These are possible answers for the questions regarding Gayle's case.

a.   The first two steps of the risk management process are identifying and analyzing loss exposures. To identify her loss exposures, Gayle should create an inventory of her business personal property. She should also complete a loss control survey to help identify the business's exposure to liability losses, including the liability for injury losses to her two employees. Gayle must use her property inventory and the survey to analyze the frequency and severity of risk associated with those loss exposures. For example, one or both of her employees could be killed in an auto accident if they rode together to attend an educational seminar. This risk is relatively small, but the cost of such a loss would be severe. Because Gayle's employees may need to handle cash and other deposits and may issue claim drafts, Gayle should consider the possible frequency and severity of the employee dishonesty exposure, as well.

b.   These are possible answers for each of the techniques:

- Avoidance—To reduce the risk that both of her employees could be injured while traveling, Gayle might implement a procedure specifying that only one of her employees can be out of the office on business at a time or that they can never travel in the same vehicle.

- Loss prevention or loss reduction—Gayle should consider actions that could help to minimize losses in her agency, such as installing locks, a security system, and smoke detectors, and training her staff in emergency procedures. Developing procedures for handling cash, other deposits, and managing agency drafts could help reduce the risk of robbery or theft, including employee theft. Adequate screening of newly hired employees could also help reduce the risk of an employee dishonesty loss.

- Insurance—Gayle's risk analysis could demonstrate that she should obtain a business policy that provides coverage for her business furnishings and equipment and to cover her business liability related to clients and prospective clients that conduct business with the agency. Gayle should also consider the need for coverage for errors or omissions that she or her employees make when conducting business, and she should consider the need for business interruption insurance. Finally, she should consider the need for workers compensation coverage.

- Retention—Gayle might determine that it would be cost-effective to self-insure her business property and equipment risk and she might determine that her business's investments would enable her to retain the risk of employee theft as opposed to purchasing employee dishonesty coverage.

6-3. These are possible answers for Dave and Gloria's case.

    a. Dave and Gloria could consider insurance transfer of the additional liability they might face because of Zach's leading other teenagers on rock climbing excursions. They might consider increasing their umbrella limit of liability.

    b. Dave and Gloria might use a risk avoidance technique. They could sell the motor boat, which would enable them to eliminate the property and liability premiums they paid for the boat.

Direct Your Learning 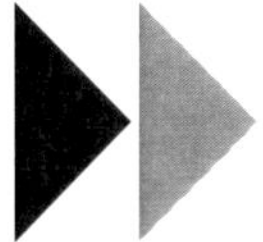

8

Loss Exposures

After learning the content of this assignment, you should be able to:

1. Describe property loss exposures in terms of assets exposed to loss, causes of loss, financial consequences of loss, and parties affected by loss.

2. Explain how legal liability to pay damages can be based on torts, contracts, or statutes.

3. Describe liability loss exposures in terms of assets exposed to loss, causes of loss, and financial consequences of loss.

4. Describe personnel loss exposures in terms of assets exposed to loss, causes of loss, and financial consequences of loss.

5. Describe net income loss exposures in terms of assets exposed to loss, causes of loss, and financial consequences of loss.

Outline

▶ **Property Loss Exposures**

  A. Assets Exposed to Property Loss
  1. Buildings
  2. Personal Property Contained in Buildings
  3. Money and Securities
  4. Vehicles and Watercraft
  5. Property in Transit
  B. Causes of Property Loss
  C. Financial Consequences of Property Losses
  D. Parties Affected by Property Losses
  1. Property Owners
  2. Secured Lenders
  3. Property Holders

▶ **The Basis for Legal Liability**

  A. Legal Foundations
  1. Sources of Law
  2. Criminal Law and Civil Law
  3. Damages
  B. Torts
  1. Negligence
  2. Intentional Torts
  3. Strict Liability
  C. Contracts
  D. Statutes

▶ **Liability Loss Exposures**

  A. Assets Exposed to Liability Loss
  B. Causes of Liability Loss
  1. Autos, Watercraft, and Other Vehicles
  2. Premises
  3. Personal Activities
  4. Business Operations
  5. Completed Operations
  6. Products
  7. Advertising
  8. Pollution
  9. Liquor
  10. Professional Activities

  C. Financial Consequences of Liability Loss
  1. Damages
  2. Defense Costs
  3. Damage to Reputation

▶ **Personnel Loss Exposures**

  A. Assets Exposed to Personnel Loss
  1. Individual Employees
  2. Owners, Officers, and Managers
  3. Groups of Employees
  B. Causes of Personnel Loss
  1. Death
  2. Disability
  3. Resignation, Layoffs, and Firing
  4. Retirement
  5. Kidnapping
  C. Financial Consequences of Personnel Losses

▶ **Net Income Loss Exposures**

  A. Assets Exposed to Net Income Loss
  B. Causes of Net Income Loss
  1. Property Loss
  2. Liability Loss
  3. Personnel Loss
  4. Business Risks
  C. Financial Consequences of Net Income Losses

Set aside a specific, realistic amount of time to study every day.

For each assignment, you should define or describe each of the Key Words and Phrases and answer each of the Review and Application Questions.

Educational Objective 1

Describe property loss exposures in terms of assets exposed to loss, causes of loss, financial consequences of loss, and parties affected by loss.

Key Words and Phrases

Fixture

Money

Securities

Auto

Mobile equipment

Recreational vehicle

Peril

Mortgagee

Mortgagor

Bailee

Review Questions

1-1. Describe the two characteristics shared by boilers and machinery.

1-2. Explain why, for insurance purposes, money and securities are separate from other types of contents.

1-3. Explain how a reduction in value might occur if repaired property is worth less than it would have been if it had never been damaged.

1-4. What does a bailee have to consider when estimating property loss exposures?

Application Question

1-5. Josh and Jill own their home. In addition to the personal property they keep within the home, they also own two vehicles.

   a. How should an insurance professional analyze Josh and Jill's property loss exposures in terms of the assets they own?

   b. How should an insurance professional analyze Josh and Jill's property loss exposures in terms of causes of loss?

   c. How should an insurance professional analyze Josh and Jill's property loss exposures in terms of financial consequences?

Educational Objective 2

Explain how legal liability to pay damages can be based on torts, contracts, or statutes.

Key Words and Phrases

Legal liability

Constitutional law

Statute

Statutory law

Common law (case law)

Criminal law

Civil law

Tort

Tort law

Negligence

Proximate cause

Tortfeasor

Vicarious liability

Intentional tort

Assault

Battery

Defamation

Slander

Libel

False arrest

Invasion of privacy

Strict liability (absolute liability)

Hold-harmless agreement (or indemnity agreement)

Warranty

Statutory liability

Review Questions

2-1. The legal system in the United States derives essentially from what three
sources of law?

2-2. To obtain a liability judgment based on negligence, what four elements must be proven?

2-3. Describe how vicarious liability often arises in business situations.

2-4. Define strict liability (absolute liability).

2-5. Explain the reason for creating statutory liability in no-fault auto insurance laws.

Application Questions

2-6. While Gary was driving his vehicle, he approached an intersection controlled by a traffic light. His light turned green, but just as he was about to enter the intersection he noticed another vehicle coming from his left through the red light. Gary abruptly halted his vehicle, narrowly missing the oncoming vehicle. If Gary asserted a liability claim against the driver of the other car would Gary likely succeed? Explain.

2-7. Renee is a physician who provided medical care to her neighbor Susan. Tess, another neighbor, asked Renee what she treated Susan for. If Renee tells Tess, could Renee be liable for committing a tort? Explain.

Educational Objective 3

Describe liability loss exposures in terms of assets exposed to loss, causes of loss, and financial consequences of loss.

Review Questions

3-1. How does the activity of ownership, maintenance, and use of an automobile rank among the other activities in terms of the number of liability claims?

3-2. Describe how a business's publication of a person using its product could lead to a lawsuit alleging invasion of privacy.

3-3. What financial consequence will defendants and their liability insurers probably incur even if all possible lawsuits are ultimately found groundless?

Application Question

3-4. Ted operates a pet shop. A customer was examining a snake when it bit him. What activity or activities would this potential liability claim arise under?

Educational Objective 4

Describe personnel loss exposures in terms of assets exposed to loss, causes of loss, and financial consequences of loss.

Key Words and Phrases

Personnel loss exposure

Key employee

Disability

Review Questions

4-1. List several reasons why an entire group of employees may leave an organiza-
tion in a short period of time.

4-2. Explain why involuntary employee separations (for example, layoffs or firings)
are not considered personnel losses.

4-3. Explain why retirement is usually not as severe a loss as death or voluntary
resignation.

Application Question

4-4. Abe is an insurance producer that owns his own agency as a sole proprietor.
After decades of working hard to build his agency, he suffered a stroke that left
him permanently and partially disabled. His doctors have told him he needs to
retire immediately.

a. Describe the insurance agency's personnel loss exposures in terms of assets exposed to personnel loss.

b. Describe the insurance agency's personnel loss exposures in terms of causes of personnel loss.

c. Describe the insurance agency's personnel loss exposures in terms of financial consequences of personnel loss.

Educational Objective 5

Describe net income loss exposures in terms of assets exposed to loss, causes of loss, and financial consequences of loss.

Review Questions

5-1. Describe the asset exposed to loss in a net income loss exposure.

5-2. Contrast a direct loss with an indirect loss.

5-3. Describe a method to determine the severity of a net income loss.

Application Question

5-4. David owns and manages a fine restaurant. Describe a potential net income loss exposure of the restaurant that may result from a property loss, a liability loss, and a personnel loss.

Answers to Assignment 8 Questions

NOTE: These answers are provided to give students a basic understanding of acceptable types of responses. They often are not the only valid answers and are not intended to provide an exhaustive response to the questions.

Educational Objective 1

1-1. These two characteristics are shared by boilers and machinery:

- They are susceptible to explosion or breakdown that can result in serious losses to the unit and to persons and property nearby.

- They are less likely to have explosions or breakdowns if they are periodically inspected and properly maintained.

1-2. For insurance purposes, money and securities are separate from other types of contents because their characteristics present special problems. Money and securities are highly susceptible to loss by theft. Cash is particularly difficult to trace because it can be readily spent. In contrast, other types of property must be sold for cash before the thief can make a profit. Money and securities are also lightweight, easily concealed, and easy to transport.

1-3. That a reduction in value might occur if repaired property is worth less than it would have been if it had never been damaged is true for items such as fine paintings and other art objects. Many collectibles are valuable largely because they are in mint or original condition. An object that has been repaired after damage from a tear, a scratch, or fire is no longer in that unspoiled condition, and its value will decline. The owner faces loss in the form of the cost to repair the object, as well as a reduction in value because of the altered condition.

1-4. Bailees are responsible for safekeeping property they do not own. Dry cleaners, repair shops, common carriers, and many other businesses temporarily hold property belonging to others. To estimate its property loss exposures, such a business has to consider not only its own property, but also the property held for others.

1-5. These answers address property loss exposures questions:

a. Insurance practitioners divide personal property into several categories: buildings, personal property contained in buildings, money and securities, vehicles and watercraft, and property in transit. Josh and Jill have a building which is their house that is exposed to loss. Their personal property contained in their home is exposed to loss. They likely also have some money and securities in the house or elsewhere that is subject to loss. Their two vehicles are subject to loss. Josh and Jill's property in transit exposure may not be as significant as the other property types but could include, for example, a set of golf clubs in the trunk of one of their vehicles while being transported to and from a golf course.

b. The building or house can be damaged or destroyed by perils such as fire, windstorm, hail, flooding, and theft. The other property types can be damaged by those perils as well. However, money and securities are particularly susceptible to loss by theft. Cash is difficult to trace because it can be readily spent. In contrast, other types of property must be sold for cash before the thief can make a profit. Money and securities are also lightweight, easily concealed, and easy to transport. Josh and Jill's vehicles and the property in transit contained in them are also exposed to the peril of collision.

c. Each type of Josh and Jill's property, if damaged or destroyed, could incur a reduction in value. If their property is damaged, the cost to repair or restore it is often the amount of reduction in value. Their property may have different values, depending on the method by which the value is determined. The most common valuation measures used in insurance policies are replacement cost and actual cash value (ACV).

Educational Objective 2

2-1. The legal system in the U.S. derives essentially from the Constitution, which is the source of constitutional law; legislative bodies, which are the sources of statutory law; and court decisions, which are the sources of common law.

2-2. These are the four elements that must be proven:

- The defendant owed a legal duty of care to the plaintiff.

- The defendant breached the duty of care owed to the plaintiff.

- The defendant's negligent act was the proximate cause of the plaintiff's injury or damage.

- The plaintiff suffered actual injury or damage.

2-3. Vicarious liability often arises in business situations from the relationship between employer and employee. An employee performing work-related activities is generally acting on behalf of the employer. Therefore, the employer can be vicariously liable for the actions of the employee.

2-4. Strict liability (absolute liability) is the legal liability arising from inherently dangerous activities or dangerously defective products that result in injury or harm to another, regardless of how much care was used in the activity.

2-5. One reason for such legislation is to ensure adequate compensation for injuries without lengthy disputes over who is at fault.

2-6. Gary would likely not succeed because a person must sustain actual harm for a liability loss to result in a valid claim.

2-7. Yes, liability for the intentional tort of invasion of privacy can arise from the unauthorized release of confidential information. Unless Susan gave Renee her consent to release her confidential medical information to another party such as Tess, Renee may be held liable if she does so.

Educational Objective 3

3-1. A significant liability loss exposure for almost all persons and businesses comes from the ownership, maintenance, and use of automobiles. In the United States, auto accidents produce the greatest number of liability claims.

3-2. Businesses often include photographs of people using their products in their advertisements. If a local retailer cannot afford professional models, it might use pictures of people using its products or shopping in its store. Unless the retailer obtains proper permission, publishing the pictures could lead to a lawsuit alleging invasion of privacy.

3-3. Even in the unlikely event that all the possible lawsuits against a defendant are ultimately found groundless, defendants and their liability insurers will probably incur substantial defense costs.

3-4. Anyone who owns or occupies real property has a premises liability loss exposure. Ted was operating a pet shop, which is the premises where the injury occurred. However, businesses must be concerned not only about the condition of their premises but also about their business operations. Whatever activity the business performs has the potential to cause harm to someone else. In this case, Ted's business operations, selling pets, resulted in an injury to a customer. So a liability claim may arise from a premises or a business operations activity.

Educational Objective 4

4-1. Over a short time period, an entire group may leave because of common dissatisfaction (such as poor management), may follow a manager to a new organization, or may be lost because of a catastrophic event.

4-2. Involuntary employee separations generally are not considered personnel losses because the organization has determined that it is better off without the employees. If, for example, a layoff is the result of a change in the organization's goals—meaning that the laid-off employees are no longer needed for the organization to operate efficiently—their departure will have a minimal effect on the organization's success. Employees are typically fired for cause (that is, for not performing their jobs effectively or behaving in an unacceptable manner).

4-3. While death and voluntary resignation often occur suddenly, retirement is usually planned. With plenty of notice, an organization can usually prepare for the retirement of even key personnel by locating and training replacements. However, as with resignation or death, when a key person decides to retire suddenly, the losses can be severe.

4-4. These answers address questions regarding the personnel case study.

a. Abe is a valuable asset of the agency because he adds value to the organization through his physical and mental labor. Abe is also a key employee because he is the owner and manager of the agency. He is responsible for making decisions essential to the agency, as well as managing and motivating others. In an organization, such as the agency, in which the owner is a key person, that person's activities, health, and managerial competence all influence the organization's value. A sole proprietorship, such as the agency, can literally cease to exist as a legal entity when its owner dies or retires. The business relationships Abe has developed with the insurers he represents and the customers he insures are also in jeopardy.

b. Abe's stroke is the cause of loss to his health. By causing a permanent disability, even if it is only partial, the cause of loss will continue until Abe can find and train a successor. Abe's sudden retirement due to the stroke may result in losses similar to the losses death or voluntary resignation would have brought.

c. Some of the financial consequences of Abe's permanent and partial disability include these:

- Loss of the value Abe contributed to the agency. (In this case, it may be severe, with the agency's value lowered at least for the short term.)

- Replacement costs (recruitment, interviewing, and training of a successor).

- Losses to the agency's value caused by negative publicity (insurers and insureds may decide to terminate their relationship with the agency).

- Losses caused by low morale of the remaining agency employees, which could result in reduced productivity and increased illness.

Educational Objective 5

5-1. The asset exposed to loss in a net income loss exposure is the future stream of net income of the individual or organization, which includes revenues minus expenses and income taxes in a given time period. If income taxes are considered to be part of an organization's expenses, a net income loss is a reduction in revenue, an increase in expenses, or a combination of the two.

5-2. A direct loss is a loss that occurs immediately as the result of a particular cause of loss, such as the reduction in the value of a building that has been damaged by fire. An indirect loss is a loss that results from, but is not directly caused by, a particular cause of loss. An example of an indirect loss would be the reduction in revenue that an organization suffers as a result of fire damage to one of its buildings.

5-3. To determine the severity of a net income loss, it is sometimes necessary to project what revenue and expenses would have been had no loss occurred. Once a loss occurs, the difference between the projected net income and the actual net income earned after the occurrence is the net income loss.

5-4. There are potential net income loss exposures for the restaurant that may result from a property loss, a liability loss, and a personnel loss.

- Property loss—A fire occurring in the kitchen of the restaurant would be a direct property loss. It would also result in a net income loss as the business could not operate without a kitchen and would have to close until it was repaired. David would not earn income from the restaurant while it was closed, which is an indirect net income loss.

- Liability loss—If a poorly maintained chair broke and dropped a customer on the floor, a resulting legal claim would be a direct liability loss. The loss of business that could occur once it became publicly known the reason the chair broke was poor maintenance would be an indirect net income loss.

- Personnel loss—The resignation of David's top chef to work for a competitor would be a personnel loss. The damage to the restaurant's reputation and loss of business would be an indirect net income loss. Another net income loss could occur if David gets in a bidding war to hire a top chef away from another competitor.

Direct Your Learning 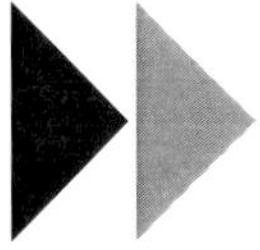

9

Insurance Policies

Educational Objectives

After learning the content of this assignment, you should be able to:

1. Explain the four elements of any valid contract.

2. Describe the distinguishing characteristics of insurance policies.

3. Explain how insurance policies can be structured using each of these alternatives:

    - Preprinted and manuscript forms

    - Self-contained and modular policies

    - Endorsements and other related documents

4. Given a specific policy provision, classify it into one of the following categories:

    - Declarations

    - Definitions

    - Insuring agreements

    - Conditions

    - Exclusions

    - Miscellaneous provisions

5. Explain how property policy provisions typically address each of the following:

    - Covered property

    - Covered locations

    - Covered causes of loss

    - Excluded causes of loss

    - Covered financial consequences

9

- Covered parties
- Amounts of recovery

6. Explain how liability policy provisions typically address each of the following:

   - Covered activities
   - Covered types of injury or damage
   - Excluded loss exposures
   - Covered costs
   - Covered time period
   - Covered parties
   - Amounts of recovery

Outline

- **Elements of a Contract**
  - A. Agreement (Offer and Acceptance)
  - B. Capacity to Contract
  - C. Consideration
  - D. Legal Purpose
- **Distinguishing Characteristics of Insurance Policies**
  - A. Contract of Indemnity
  - B. Contract of Utmost Good Faith
  - C. Contract Involving Fortuitous Events and the Exchange of Unequal Amounts
  - D. Contract of Adhesion
  - E. Conditional Contract
  - F. Nontransferable Contract
- **Insurance Policy Structure**
  - A. Preprinted and Manuscript Forms
  - B. Self-Contained and Modular Policies
  - C. Endorsements and Other Related Documents
- **Policy Provisions**
  - A. Declarations
  - B. Definitions
  - C. Insuring Agreements
  - D. Conditions
  - E. Exclusions
  - F. Miscellaneous Provisions
- **Property Policy Provisions**
  - A. Covered Property
  - B. Covered Locations
  - C. Covered Causes of Loss
  - D. Excluded Causes of Loss
  - E. Covered Financial Consequences
  - F. Covered Parties
  - G. Amounts of Recovery
- **Liability Policy Provisions**
  - A. Covered Activities
  - B. Covered Types of Injury or Damage
    1. Bodily Injury
    2. Property Damage
    3. Personal and Advertising Injury
  - C. Excluded Loss Exposures
  - D. Covered Costs
    1. Damages
    2. Defense Costs
    3. Supplementary Payments
    4. Medical Payments
  - E. Covered Time Period
  - F. Covered Parties
  - G. Amounts of Recovery
    1. Policy Limits
    2. Defense Cost Provisions
    3. "Other Insurance" Provisions

Writing notes as you read your materials will help you remember key pieces of information.

For each assignment, you should define or describe each of the Key Words and Phrases and answer each of the Review and Application Questions.

Educational Objective 1
Explain the four elements of any valid contract.

Key Words and Phrases

Valid contract

Consideration

Review Questions

1-1. Describe when the process of achieving mutual assent in insurance generally begins.

1-2. Describe what could occur if an insurer mistakenly writes an insurance policy in a state where that insurer is not licensed.

1-3. In an insurance contract, describe the insurer's consideration.

Application Questions

1-4. Despite being a minor, Ralph completes an auto insurance application and sends it to an underwriter of an insurer. The underwriter accepts his application. Later when the insurer tries to collect the premium it earned by providing coverage to Ralph, he claims he does not owe it because the contract is not enforceable. Is Ralph correct? Explain.

1-5. Edgar was behind on his car payments and drove his car into a lake. He contacted the police and his auto insurance claims representative to inform them his car was stolen. The car was later recovered and the evidence indicated Edgar caused the damage to his vehicle. How does Edgar's action affect the insurance contract's legal purpose?

Educational Objective 2
Describe the distinguishing characteristics of insurance policies.

Key Words and Phrases

Principle of indemnity

Valued policy

Concealment

Misrepresentation

Material fact

Conditional contract

Review Questions

2-1. List the six distinct characteristics of an insurance policy.

2-2. Explain how a contract of indemnity does not necessarily pay the full amount necessary to restore an insured who has suffered a covered loss to the same financial position.

2-3. Why is insurance considered a contract of utmost good faith?

2-4. What is the distinction between concealment and misrepresentation?

2-5. Insurance buyers agree to pay a premium, and insurers agree to pay claims. Why does this contract involve an exchange of unequal amounts?

Application Question

2-6. An insured who has recently been involved in a minor auto accident states, "I have been driving for years and never had an auto accident. Now I finally have a chance to get back those thousands of dollars of premiums I have paid, so I am going to take the insurer for everything I can get." Explain why this person has a misconception concerning how insurance policies are designed to work.

Educational Objective 3

Explain how insurance policies can be structured using each of these alternatives:

- **Preprinted and manuscript forms**
- **Self-contained and modular policies**
- **Endorsements and other related documents**

Key Words and Phrases

Preprinted form

Manuscript form

Coverage part

Declarations page (declarations, or dec.)

Endorsement

Review Questions

3-1. Explain how preprinted policy forms and manuscript policy forms differ.

3-2. Describe the information typically contained in an insurance application and explain how that information is used by an insurer.

3-3. Explain how coverage is determined in a policy in which an endorsement conflicts with the original policy provisions.

Application Question

3-4. The Boom Company manufactures sparklers and fireworks used for community Fourth of July celebrations. It recently expanded operations and purchased an additional warehouse for inventory storage. Explain what type of form would likely be used by the insurer to cover all of Boom's coverage needs.

Educational Objective 4

Given a specific policy provision, classify it into one of the following categories:

- **Declarations**
- **Definitions**
- **Insuring agreements**
- **Conditions**
- **Exclusions**
- **Miscellaneous provisions**

Key Words and Phrases

Policy provision

Scheduled coverage

Insuring agreement

Condition

Exclusion

Review Questions

4-1. List six common categories of policy provisions found in insurance policies.

4-2. Describe the purpose of a policy insuring agreement.

4-3. Identify the obligations of these parties as stated in the conditions of an insurance policy:

a. Insurer

b. Insured

4-4. List the purposes of exclusions in an insurance policy.

4-5. Identify loss exposures typically excluded from a policy because they are considered uninsurable.

Application Question

4-6. Jane is in an auto accident while driving her insured car. Her son, John, a passenger, is injured. Jane is wondering whether John is an insured under the medical payments coverage of her auto policy. What section of the policy would clarify the term "insured" and help determine whether John is considered an insured under the policy?

Educational Objective 5

Explain how property policy provisions typically address each of the following:

- **Covered property**
- **Covered locations**
- **Covered causes of loss**
- **Excluded causes of loss**
- **Covered financial consequences**
- **Covered parties**
- **Amounts of recovery**

Key Words and Phrases

Floater

Named peril

Special form, or open perils policy

Collision coverage

Other than collision (OTC) coverage

Specified causes of loss coverage

Direct loss

Time element loss (indirect loss)

Net income

Extra expenses

Additional living expense (ALE)

Named insured

Loss payee

Deductible

Insurance-to-value provision

Coinsurance

Review Questions

5-1. Explain why exclusions and limitations are not the same thing.

5-2. Explain why a property insurance policy for covering personal property that moves from one place to another is often called a floater.

5-3. Explain why some perils that affect many people at the same time are generally considered to be uninsurable.

5-4. Explain why a business incurs extra expenses after experiencing a direct property loss.

5-5.   Describe the purposes of a policy limit.

5-6.   Explain why property insurance policies usually contain a deductible provision.

Application Questions

5-7.   Peter owns an older home with a plumbing system that, over the years, has become prone to developing leaks. He is on a tight budget and needs to save money wherever possible, including in the amount of insurance premium he pays. He is trying to decide which policy form (basic, broad, or special) he should buy to insure his house. Which policy form would probably best fit Peter's needs? Explain.

5-8. Mary owns a duplex. She lives in one unit and rents out the other. She has explained to her agent that she needs the rental income from the other unit every month in order to pay the mortgage. If the rental unit was uninhabitable because of a fire, for example, she would lose her home. What assurance can her agent provide her about this risk when discussing the coverage provided in a homeowners policy?

Educational Objective 6

Explain how liability policy provisions typically address each of the following:

- **Covered activities**
- **Covered types of injury or damage**
- **Excluded loss exposures**
- **Covered costs**
- **Covered time period**
- **Covered parties**
- **Amounts of recovery**

Key Words and Phrases

Bodily injury

Property damage

Personal injury

Release

Supplementary payments

Prejudgment interest

Postjudgment interest

Medical payments coverage

Occurrence basis coverage

Claims-made coverage form

Retroactive date

Each person limit

Each occurrence limit

Aggregate limit

Split limits

Single limit

Review Questions

6-1. Describe the two approaches used by liability insurance policies to define covered activities.

6-2. Describe what advertising injury, as covered by most commercial general liability (CGL) policies, typically includes.

6-3. Explain how pollution exclusions help keep premiums reasonable.

6-4. Explain why some states do not permit insurers to pay punitive damages on behalf of their insureds.

6-5. Explain how a liability policy with a single limit applies to a loss involving property damage and bodily injury to multiple individuals.

Application Questions

6-6. According to both CGL and homeowners policies, property damage includes both direct losses and time element (or indirect) losses sustained by the claimant. If a delicatessen has to close for twenty days because of water damage caused by a leaking pipe from the business next door, what are the restaurant's direct and time element (or indirect) losses?

6-7. Larry recently bought a small plane for personal use. He damaged another party's parked plane when he accidently collided with it. Larry reported the claim to his homeowner's insurer who told him there was no coverage. Explain why the homeowners policy does not cover this loss.

6-8. Fran was injured in two unrelated accidents. She was injured the first time when she hit her head in an auto accident, and the second time when she slipped and fell in her kitchen. She has both personal auto and homeowners insurance with the same insurer. She files a claim for medical payments for both injuries. Explain how Fran's personal auto and homeowners insurance will or will not cover each medical payment claim.

Answers to Assignment 9 Questions

NOTE: These answers are provided to give students a basic understanding of acceptable types of responses. They often are not the only valid answers and are not intended to provide an exhaustive response to the questions.

Educational Objective 1

1-1.   In insurance, the process of achieving mutual assent generally begins when someone who wants to purchase insurance completes an insurance application—an offer to buy insurance. The details on the application describe the exposures to be insured and indicate the coverage the applicant requests.

1-2.   If an insurer mistakenly writes an insurance policy in a state where that insurer is not licensed, the insured might later argue that the contract is not valid and demand the return of the premium. This demand would be based on the fact that the insurer did not have the legal capacity to make the agreement.

1-3.   In an insurance contract, the insurer's consideration is its promise to pay a claim in the future if a covered loss occurs. If no loss occurs, the insurer is still fulfilling its promise to provide financial protection even though it does not pay a claim.

1-4.   Being a minor can remove capacity of an individual to contract causing the contract to be un-enforceable. However, minors are sometimes considered competent to purchase auto insurance, especially when auto insurance qualifies as a necessity. State laws vary in regard to issues involving minors. If Ralph applied for the insurance in a state that recognizes auto insurance as a necessity, he may owe the premium being billed by the insurer.

1-5.   No insurance contract will remain valid if the wrongful conduct of the insured causes the operation of the contract to violate public policy. So, by intentionally driving his car into the lake, Edgar rendered his auto insurance policy unenforceable and would preclude his recovery under his policy for the damage he intentionally caused.

Educational Objective 2

2-1.   An insurance policy is a contract of indemnity, a contract of the utmost good faith, a contract involving fortuitous events and the exchange of unequal amounts, a contract of adhesion, a conditional contract, and a nontransferable contract.

2-2.   Most policies contain a policy limit that specifies the maximum amount the insurer will pay for a single claim. Many policies also contain limitations and other provisions that could reduce the amount of recovery. For example, a homeowners policy is not designed to cover large amounts of cash. Therefore, most homeowners policies contain a special limit, such as $200, for any covered loss to money owned by the insured. In that instance, if a covered fire destroys $1,000 in cash belonging to the insured, the insurer will pay only $200 for the money that was destroyed.

2-3.   Insurance is considered a contract of utmost good faith because insurance involves a promise that requires complete honesty and disclosure of all relevant facts from both parties. Both parties to an insurance contract—the insurer and the insured—are expected to be ethical in their dealings with each other.

2-4. The distinction between concealment and misrepresentation is that concealment is an intentional failure to disclose a material fact (omission) but a misrepresentation is a false statement of a material fact (falsehood).

2-5. The insurance contract involves an exchange of unequal amounts because, often, there are few or no losses and the premium paid by the insured for a particular policy is more than the amount paid by the insurer to, or on behalf of, the insured. If a large loss occurs, however, the insurer's claim payment might be much more than the premium paid by the insured. It is the possibility that the insurer's obligation might be much greater than the insured's that makes the insurance transaction a fair trade.

2-6. This insured does not understand that an auto policy is designed to work as a contract involving the exchange of unequal amounts. The premium paid by the insured for a particular policy can be, and often is, more than the amount paid by the insurer to, or on behalf of, the insured for a covered loss. The contract is also designed to work as a conditional contract. The insurer must perform only under certain conditions, such as when a covered loss occurs during the policy period. A covered loss might not occur during a particular policy period, but that fact does not mean the insurance policy for that period has been worthless. In buying an insurance policy, the insured acquires a valuable promise—the promise of the insurer to make payments if a covered loss occurs. The promise exists, even if the insurer's performance is not required during the policy period.

Educational Objective 3

3-1. Preprinted policy forms are standardized contracts developed for different types of insurance that do not require negotiating new contractual terms for each policy purchased. Manuscript policy forms are customized contracts developed for a specific insured or group of insureds who share unique coverage needs.

3-2. An insurance application typically contains information about the insured and the loss exposures presented to the insurer.

3-3. If the policy and the endorsement contain conflicting terms, the endorsement takes precedence.

3-4. The insurer would likely use a manuscript policy for Boom's insurance contract because the company's coverage needs are specialized due to the explosive nature of its manufactured items. Typically, the insurer would not have standard forms available to cover this exposure and would have to customize the policy for the Boom's specific coverage needs.

Educational Objective 4

4-1. These are six categories of policy provisions found in insurance policies:

- Declarations
- Definitions
- Insuring agreements
- Conditions
- Exclusions
- Miscellaneous provisions

4-2. The purpose of a policy insuring agreement is to state in broad terms the insurer's promises to the insured.

4-3. These are the obligations of the parties as stated in the conditions of an insurance policy:

   a. Obligations of the insurer as stated in the conditions of an insurance policy are to pay covered losses, to defend the insured from lawsuits, and to provide other services to the insured.

   b. Obligations of the insured that are commonly stated in the conditions of an insurance policy are to pay premiums; to report losses promptly; to provide appropriate documentation for losses; to cooperate with the insurer, as in legal proceedings; and to refrain from jeopardizing an insurer's rights to recover from responsible third parties (subrogate).

4-4. Exclusions in an insurance policy can serve one or more purposes:

   - Eliminate coverage for uninsurable loss exposures

   - Assist in managing moral hazards

   - Assist in managing morale hazards

   - Reduce the likelihood of coverage duplications

   - Eliminate coverages that the typical insured does not need

   - Eliminate coverages requiring special treatment

   - Assist in keeping premiums reasonable

4-5. Loss exposures typically excluded from a policy because they are considered uninsurable include nonaccidental events such as war, earthquake, or flood.

4-6. The definitions section helps clarify terms that have specific meaning within Jane's auto policy. The definition of the term "insured" in that section may help verify whether John is covered under the policy.

Educational Objective 5

5-1. While exclusions eliminate all coverage for excluded property or causes of loss, limitations place a specific dollar limit on specific property that is covered.

5-2. A property insurance policy for covering personal property that moves from one place to another is often called a floater because it provides coverage that floats, or moves, with the property as it changes location.

5-3. Some perils that affect many people at the same time are generally considered to be uninsurable because the resulting losses would be so widespread that the funds of the entire insurance business might be inadequate to pay all of the claims. For this reason, almost all property insurance policies exclude coverage for losses from catastrophes such as war and nuclear hazard.

5-4. The reason a business incurs extra expenses after experiencing a direct property loss is to continue its operations, which may also reduce the business income loss.

5-5. A policy limit has several purposes. It tells the insured the maximum amount of money that can be recovered from the insurer after a loss. By comparing the policy limit to the value that may be lost, the insured can determine whether the amount of insurance is adequate. The policy limit is also important because it allows insurers to keep track of their overall obligations in any one geographic area and because the premium charged is directly related to the policy limit for most property insurance coverages.

5-6. Property insurance policies usually contain a deductible provision, which serves several functions. Deductibles encourage the insured to try to prevent losses because the insured will bear a part of any loss. Shifting the cost of small claims to the insured also enables the insurer to reduce premiums. Handling claims for small amounts often costs more than the dollar amount of the claim. Thus, deductibles enable people to purchase coverage for serious losses at a reasonable price without unnecessarily involving the insurer in small losses.

5-7. The basic form covers the fewest perils of the three forms and therefore has the lowest premium. However, the basic form does not cover sudden and accidental leakage of water from a plumbing system. Therefore, the basic form is probably not the form best suited for Peter. The broad form covers more perils than the basic form but fewer than the special form. The broad form's premium is likely higher than the basic form's, yet lower than the special form's. The broad form does cover the peril of sudden and accidental leakage of water from a plumbing system, so it is probably the best choice for Peter.

5-8. Her agent could explain that homeowners policies provide coverage for lost income. When a covered cause of loss, such as a fire, damages the part of a residence that Mary rents or holds for rental to others, "fair rental value" coverage in the homeowners policy indemnifies her for the loss of rental income until the rented portion of the residence has been restored to livable condition.

Educational Objective 6

6-1. Liability insurance policies use two approaches to defining covered activities. Certain policies state the specific activity or source of liability covered, such as an auto insurance liability policy stating that it applies to claims that result from covered auto accidents. General liability insurance, in contrast, covers all activities or sources of liability that are not specifically excluded.

6-2. Advertising injury, which is covered by most CGL policies, typically includes libel and slander; publication of material that constitutes an invasion of privacy; misappropriation of advertising ideas or business style; and infringement of copyright, trade dress, or slogan.

6-3. Commercial liability policies generally exclude all but limited exposures from pollution. Businesses with more serious pollution liability exposures must purchase specialty policies to cover those exposures. If broad pollution coverage were provided under all liability policies, the coverage would not be affordable.

6-4. Some states do not permit insurers to pay punitive damages because the punishment is viewed as less effective if the responsible party does not personally pay the required damages.

6-5. The most an insurer will pay is the combined single limit for all property damage and bodily injury to which the insurance applies; regardless of the number of persons injured. A single limit applies to any combination of bodily injury and property damage liability claims arising from the same occurrence. For example, a \$300,000 single limit covers a bodily injury loss up to \$300,000, a property damage liability loss up to \$300,000, or any combination of bodily injury and property damage arising from a single occurrence up to \$300,000.

6-6. The direct losses include the cost of repairing the water damage to the delicatessen's property, which may also include replacing some inventory. The time element (or indirect) losses include the loss of income for the twenty days that the delicatessen had to be closed for repairs.

6-7. No insurance policy can reasonably cover all loss exposures. Liability insurance policies generally follow the broad guideline to eliminate duplicate coverage provided by policies specifically designed to address particular exposures such as aircraft liability. Larry should have bought a separate policy that specifically covers aircraft liability.

6-8. Personal auto policy medical payments coverage will cover her as an insured for her head injury, up to a specified limit. However, her homeowners policy's medical payments coverage will not cover her slip-and-fall injury because she is an insured or regular resident of her household.

Exam Information

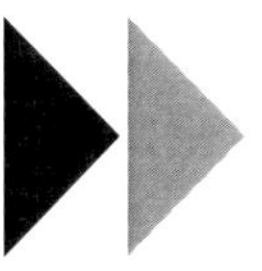

About Institutes Exams

Exam questions are based on the Educational Objectives stated in the course guide and textbook. The exam is designed to measure whether you have met those Educational Objectives. The exam does not necessarily test every Educational Objective. It tests over a balanced sample of Educational Objectives.

How to Prepare for Institutes Exams

What can you do to prepare for an Institutes exam? Students who pass Institutes exams do the following:

▶ Use the assigned study materials. Focus your study on the Educational Objectives presented at the beginning of each course guide assignment. Thoroughly read the textbook and any other assigned materials, and then complete the course guide exercises. Choose a study method that best suits your needs; for example, participate in a traditional class, online class, or informal study group; or study on your own. Use The Institutes' SMART Study Aids (if available) for practice and review. If this course has an associated SMART Online Practice Exams product, you will find an access code on the inside back cover of this course guide. This access code allows you to print a full practice exam and to take additional online practice exams that will simulate an actual credentialing exam.

▶ Become familiar with the types of test questions asked on the exam. The practice exam in this course guide or in the SMART Online Practice Exams product will help you understand the different types of questions you will encounter on the exam.

▶ Maximize your test-taking time. Successful students use the sample exam in the course guide or in the SMART Online Practice Exams product to practice pacing themselves. Learning how to manage your time during the exam ensures that you will complete all of the test questions in the time allotted.

Types of Exam Questions

The exam for this course consists of objective questions of several types.

The Correct-Answer Type

In this type of question, the question stem is followed by four responses, one of which is absolutely correct. Select the *correct* answer.

> Which one of the following persons evaluates requests for insurance to determine which applicants are accepted and which are rejected?
>
> a.   The premium auditor
>
> b.   The loss control representative
>
> c.   The underwriter
>
> d.   The risk manager

The Best-Answer Type

In this type of question, the question stem is followed by four responses, only one of which is best, given the statement made or facts provided in the stem. Select the *best* answer.

> Several people within an insurer might be involved in determining whether an applicant for insurance is accepted. Which one of the following positions is primarily responsible for determining whether an applicant for insurance is accepted?
>
> a.   The loss control representative
>
> b.   The customer service representative
>
> c.   The underwriter
>
> d.   The premium auditor

The Incomplete-Statement or Sentence-Completion Type

In this type of question, the last part of the question stem consists of a portion of a statement rather than a direct question. Select the phrase that *correctly* or *best* completes the sentence.

Residual market plans designed for individuals who are unable to obtain insurance on their personal property in the voluntary market are called

a. VIN plans.

b. Self-insured retention plans.

c. Premium discount plans.

d. FAIR plans.

"All of the Above" Type

In this type of question, only one of the first three answers could be correct, or all three might be correct, in which case the best answer would be "All of the above." Read all the answers and select the *best* answer.

When a large commercial insured's policy is up for renewal, who is likely to provide input to the renewal decision process?

a. The underwriter

b. The loss control representative

c. The producer

d. All of the above

"All of the following, EXCEPT:" Type

In this type of question, responses include three correct answers and one answer that is incorrect or is clearly the least correct. Select the *incorrect* or *least correct* answer.

All of the following adjust insurance claims, EXCEPT:

a. Insurer claims representatives

b. Premium auditors

c. Producers

d. Independent adjusters